WALKING WITH DOGS

IN

HEREFORDSHIRE IN WALES

A Walk along *Vaughan's Way*, linking the *Offa's Dyke Path*
with the *Wye Valley Walk*, Kington to Bredwardine,
with some alternative circular additions.

R.W.D.Fenn and S.T.J.Fenn

With a foreword by
Jilly Cooper

Illustrated by
P.L.Willmer

MID-BORDER BOOKS
CASTLE HILL HOUSE
KINGTON
TEL: [01544] 231195 FAX [01544] 231161

CONTENTS

[On back cover: The Authors and Illustrator]

FOREWORD

Jilly Cooper

On the all too few occasions when I have visited *Herefordshire in Wales*, I have felt a flicker of guilty infidelity that the country there is even more beautiful than my beloved Gloucestershire.

Where else do rivers idle more seductively along deep green valleys or trees soar upwards more proudly as if they alone propped up the sky?

How much more rewarding then to wander through this bewitching countryside with a book like *Walking with a Greyhound* to explain the history and poetry in which it is steeped.

I was fascinated for example to learn that truancy was just as rife in Bredwardine in the early 19th Century as it is today, with pupils always sloping off to hop-pick, follow the hunt or enjoy a visiting fair. Predictable too that Governments were just as stingy. Having benevolently bestowed a mere £670 so that a school for 80 pupils might be built in Almeley in 1850, the Government insisted on having it back afterwards.

The book is also crammed with thrilling *News of the World* stories of Herefordshire's vicars rigging elections, peers murdering their father-in-laws, and nineteen year old heirs running off with thirteen-year old girls, before going clean off their heads. And I was amused by the bellringers of Almeley who after their exertions would pour into the nearest local, for free booze, which would subsequently be recorded in the church accounts as 'drink for my trouble'.

It also adds to the enjoyment of a walk to know there are ferns and wildflowers in the dingle ahead, the bottle brush plant in the next field, that the next bank will be thick and scented in summer with wild rose and honeysuckle or that round the corner is a wonderful view of the Black Mountains.

When we first moved to Gloucestershire, walking my dogs was a nightmare. I didn't know where to go, and was always spiking myself clambering over barbed wire, being chased by cows and shouted at for trespassing by angry farmers. If only I had this book to hand which warns you in advance where to find the right footpath and where you will be expected to keep your dogs on a lead or hoist them over stiles, not much fun in the case of our rotund black labrador described last week by a roadworker as 'even wider than the Water Board'.

You will also be provided with useful tips about where bullocks are likely to breathe down your neck, or where you'll pass a garden of hysterically barking dogs or might even see a Persian cat (regarded as High Tea by my dogs) sitting on a bridge.

All this invaluable information is included because Gabby the beautiful black greyhound of the title enjoyed and test-marketed all the walks written about.

Gabby, who is the heroine of the book, suffered a dark and dreadful past before she came to live with co-author Sebastian Fenn. Like other greyhounds considered past their best, or not quite fast enough for the tracks in England and Ireland, she was sold to the Spanish who keep their dogs in appalling conditions and race them into the ground. Once these gentle creatures can give no more, an even more dreadful fate may await them. They are taken deep into the woods, strung up from trees, and the Spaniards have bets on which dog will die first.

Thank God for Anne Finch, another heroine as pretty as she is brave, who has rescued many of these greyhounds including Gabby, from such a hideous end, putting them often through quarantine and into the hands of another brave and pretty woman, Angela Collett at Greyhound Rescue, West of England, who rehomes them in this country.

I too have a rescued lurcher, who is at least seven eighths greyhound, called Hero. When she was a puppy, Hero, her mother and her two sisters were found in a sack tied to a stone at the bottom of a river. Ten and a half years later, she is still fearful and timid with strangers.

Nothing however equals her welcome - pirouetting in ecstasy like Darcy Bussell - for members of the family or my joy at taking her for walks: seeing her bounding, tail rotating across the lawn or going berserk in the long russet grasses in the twilight on summer evenings.

Best of all she loves, like all her breed, to run - hanging back pretending to look for rabbits so she can build up a distance of a couple of hundred yards. Suddenly there is a thunder of paws, as she catches up, collapsing, onyx eyes shining in delight at my feet. I could go on for hours on the pleasure of owning these droll, affectionate dogs.

Finally there is the joy of walking itself. Every day in all weathers it restores my sanity and lifts my heart. It is the best way of reducing stress and it costs nothing. 'The birds in the trees sing for rich and poor' wrote Sacheverell Sitwell.

Roy and Seb Fenn, the authors of this charming book, are therefore owed a great debt of gratitude. Unearthing so much historical, geographical and practical detail and presenting it so interestingly must have taken months, even years of hard work. Their only reward has been the thrill of discovery, because all their royalties will go towards Greyhound Rescue, West of England.

Once you have bought your copy, therefore, I beg you to buy more to hand out to friends, ensuring them days of pleasure and adventure – and with luck they might even decide to adopt a greyhound.

WALKING WITH A GREYHOUND

INTRODUCTION

This book was written during the late summer and early autumn of 2001 when the prolonged foot and mouth epidemic had subsided. Peter Newman of the Open Spaces Society commissioned it, and his indefatigable labours to keep open and define the public footpaths and rights of way of Herefordshire, thereby making the beauty of its landscape more accessible to all, are well known.

Why did we limit the scope of the book to *Herefordshire in Wales*, wherever that might be? It is that part of Herefordshire, *west* of Offa's dyke, which we, father and son, know best. We are fascinated as much by its history as by its landscape. The Welsh bards of Powys spoke of it as being 'the backside of paradise', believing, of course, that they lived in paradise itself. The truth of this description is self-evident.

The historical interest of the area lies in its being the meeting place, and at times the battle ground, of landscapes, cultures, languages, and values. Rushing streams flow down to the gently flowing Wye, upland farming mingles with its lowland counterpart, buildings of stone give way to those which are timber framed, and little whitewashed hillside churches dedicated to the Celtic saints of the Dark Ages are displaced by the great Saxon minsters of Leominster and Hereford.

Welsh surnames abound in the local telephone directory, and none more so than that of the Vaughans who for centuries were pre-eminent in our local history. It was the Welsh speaking Vaughans of Hergest and Bredwardine who kept open house for the Welsh bards; a Vaughan was the foundress in 1621 of Lady Hawkins' School in Kington, which with its famous library, offered the farmers' sons the best in education then available. The Vaughans represented both sides of the border in Parliament, and were sheriffs and magistrates as often in Herefordshire as in Radnorshire. Frequently in these walks we suggest the reader should turn and facing west, look towards the Black Mountains and the Brecon Beacons, celebrated in the mystical poetry of the best known of the Vaughans, Henry Vaughan the Silurist. It was he, who, brought up amongst this landscape, wrote that he had seen eternity, and in the troubled times of the Civil War, spoke of another country, far above the stars.

1

In writing our book, we had two groups of walkers particularly in mind. Firstly, there are those who walk solely for the pleasure of walking. For them there are for each walk directions and a plan of the route, everything else can be safely skipped. Our original brief was to write a guide for a linear walk simply linking Kington, where *Mortimer's Trail* comes to an end, with Bredwardine, where the *Wye Valley Trail* can be joined. And this can still be done, but it seemed better and more interesting to offer some variations, each complete in itself, on this theme. Indeed, it is possible for the truly stout hearted to undertake a circular walk, from Kington to Kington, via Almeley and Bredwardine.

Secondly, there are those who have a taste for history and like to know something about the countryside through which they walk. They will want to stop and look at churches and farm houses, read inscriptions on monuments and ponder the archaeology, and we hope what is said about these things in the book will enrich their enjoyment.

We also had another group in mind, which despite their intelligence, are quite unable to read our words. These are the dogs that benefit from the voluntary efforts on their behalf of Greyhound Rescue West of England. The authors' royalties are being donated to this registered charity. Gabby, a greyhound rescued from horrendous experiences in Ireland and Spain, related elsewhere in this book, accompanied us on all the walks.

There is a glossary of what may be to some unfamiliar terms, a bibliography for those who want to read more about the places we visited, and an index, which can be useful because when parts of a walk are covered elsewhere we have avoided duplicating the historical material. Our debt to the late Nikolaus Pevsner, the doyen of 20th century architectural historians, will be obvious. We made great use, too, of the notes made in 1863 when the learned members of the Cambrian Archaeological Association, fully aware of the concept and locality of *Herefordshire in Wales* came to Kington for their annual summer conference. Travelling in horse drawn wagonettes, like us, they visited Almeley, Bredwardine, Bollingham, and Eardisley and their account of what they saw and found interesting in comparison with what later commentators have written, offers an interesting insight to Victorian values and taste.

We have walked all the walks ourselves, and experience has shown that the nearer you get to Almeley, the more frequently stiles with dog bars occur. Otherwise it is a matter of lifting the unfortunate canine over the stile, since most of the stiles which are not dog friendly have wire netting to stop animals getting through the lower bars. Gabby, our accompanying greyhound, seemed to get progressively heavier as the walks went on. Hats are a good idea, brambles and branches can inflict painful wounds upon the scalp, however well protected by a fine head of hair. And there is too the danger of sunburn. Stout boots and a stick are almost essential, because even on the hottest days, pockets of oozing mud will always turn up. A mobile telephone is not to be despised, just in case.

Do please use a large scale Ordnance Survey Map.

Our thanks are due to Peter Newman for commissioning the book, to Lawrence Banks of Ridgebourne and the Hergest Trust, for allowing us the free use of the Banks Archives for our research, to Jim Sinclair for taking the photographs from which the illustrator worked, and, most of all, to you our readers for helping our cause by buying the book.

Happy walking, happy history.

RWD Fenn
STJ Fenn

December 2001

GABBY: WHO IS SHE?

Gabby the greyhound was born somewhere in Ireland in 1993. She presumably had a racing career of some sorts but either wasn't fast enough or became too old, because she was sold to the Mallorca track in Spain where she was known as *Delicias*. It is believed that upwards of 12,000 greyhounds a year 'leave' the racing industry in one way or another, so going to Spain is not uncommon. Whilst this development was literally a stay of execution for Gabby, her life was little easier. Greyhounds are treated particularly badly in Spain, being made to run excessive numbers of races with minimal veterinary care, and in poor living conditions.

Gabby proved to be exceptionally lucky, however, and was rescued by Anne Finch and her charity *Greyhounds In Need*. This charity is dedicated to improving the plight of racing greyhounds and the native hunting greyhounds, the *Galgos*, in Spain. Typically this means removing the dogs from Spain and sending then across Europe or even to America.

For Gabby in pre-pet passport times, this necessitated a six months period of quarantine in Dover. On completion of this, she was handed over to *Greyhound Rescue West of England*, a charity devoted to the rescue and rehabilitation of abused and abandoned greyhounds. Gabby's travels were completed in September 1999 when she came to live with her present owners in Gloucester.

She is typical of her breed in many ways. For example, she is very affectionate, classically lazy and impossible to remove from the sofa once she has made it her throne for the day. It did, however, take her some time to settle into domestic life. Slippery floors and patio doors can still catch her out, although stairs are no problem, and she instinctively knows that beds are for sleeping on, come the hours of darkness.

Two half-hour walks are normally sufficient for her, despite the common misconception that greyhounds need lots of exercise. Thus Gabby was secretly glad of the leisurely pace enforced by the more mature of her two human companions on these walks.

Charming though she is, she does have her foibles. It would be nice if she didn't shred any paper that is left unattended in the house or eat all the chocolate Christmas decorations. Nevertheless, Gabby's owners hope that her retirement will be a long one, and that there are many more walks in the countryside to come.

Gabby is not the first greyhound to have walked the bounds of Kington, her predecessors, however, had to earn their keep, and they like Gabby, were no strangers to cruelty. The *Diaries* of Thomas Skarratt,1819-1909, the Kington draper, tell how in October 1853 on 'a bright and healthy morning' he went with his brother William and the greyhounds to meet Mr John Price of Hergest Court. They 'killed three hares and came home very tired'. In January 1854 Skarratt 'went for a walk with the greyhounds. Ran one hare and lost her in the gorse'. But six months later he wrote:

> Some kindly-disposed 'Friend' poisoned my old greyhound *Pilot*. So strong was the dose that death ensued in five minutes after he was taken ill.

But Pilot had his successors and in November 1881 Skarratt heard from a kinsman:

> Received a few lines from Chas. to say he would be in Hereford this evening in time for the draw of Greyhounds for the Bredwardine Coursing Meeting on the morrow and would see me there.

As we walked up Bredwardine Hill, with Gabby sniffing the air, and her ears erect, could she scent and hear her predecessors along that way?

————————

More information on Greyhound Rescue West of England can be obtained using the Helpline (07000 785092).

KINGTON

The place-name Kington makes its first recorded appearance in 1086 in Domesday, though the actual foundation of Kington as a small borough built around its protecting castle seems to belong to the early years of King Henry I, who reigned 1100-1135. Several factors commended the manor of Kington for such a role. It was both defensible against Welsh attack and could command the valley approach into Wales between Bradnor Hill and Hergest Ridge. It could control the crossing of the Arrow, which was not always a benign stream and could flood into a substantial torrent. It was the meeting place of five established track ways, to New Radnor, Brilley, Presteign, Leominster, and Hereford; its position was ideal for a market which would bring tolls to the lord and prosperity for the burghers of his borough. The truth of this is illustrated by the survival to the present day of Kington market at the expense of those of New Radnor and Presteign.

As one would expect, *Herefordshire in Wales*, has its place in Welsh culture and tradition. In the late medieval period Hergest Court, in the parish of Kington, was the home of the Vaughans and a great centre of Welsh culture and bardic poetry. These bards spoke of Powys as the Paradise of Wales: and by analogy saw Herefordshire as being nothing less than the backside of Paradise. Welsh place names survive locally and remind the visitor that Welsh was once the predominant language: Hergest and Penrhos are obviously Welsh, Arrow and Lilwall less obviously so. The name of the River Arrow is related to the Welsh word for silver, *arian*, and Lilwall is derived ultimately from the Welsh personal name Llywelyn, which in turn incorporates the element *llelo*, a fool.

Kington's nineteenth century bank was called the *Kington and Radnorshire Bank* and the present day hunt, with an equal disregard for national frontiers, is called the *Radnorshire and West Hereford*. Though it never achieved the civic status of a borough, as did its nearby Radnorshire rivals of Presteign and New Radnor, it prospered at their expense. Its weekly market and annual sheep sales are still important; its seventeenth century grammar school still flourishes in its comprehensive guise; its local quarries famous since the early nineteenth century for their lime and grit stone are now part of an international company. The local population enjoys enviable access to the latest information technology through having its own community computer centre.

The town of Kington has been served well both by its local gentry, like the Vaughans of Hergest Court, patrons of the medieval bards and prominent in seventeenth century Welsh politics and by incomers of initiative and enterprise like the Bankses of Ridgebourne who are still prominent in the town's life. Its tradesmen have also enhanced its prosperity and Mr AW Gamage who was once in business at 13 High Street founded the famous London firm that bore his name. National figures like James Watt the famous engineer have played their part too. In the course of the nineteenth century Kington became the centre of a miniature network of railways, all of which were established by a local collaboration of gentry and tradesmen.

Walk 1: Kington to Almeley

Our walk starts in Mill Street at the *Tourist and Information Centre*, open daily in the tourist season 10-1 and 2-5. As you turn right on leaving the *Centre,* cast an eye to the other side of the street to your left where you will see Kington Museum. It opened in 1986 and is housed in what were once the stables of the *King's Head,* in its day one of the principal inns in the town. The Market Hall now stands on its site. Later on these stables accommodated the horse for the municipal dust cart, before that became motorised, then for a while it was the home of the town's ambulance. Its extensions were opened in 1991 by a descendant of Thomas Skarratt, 1818-1909, the Kington diarist and clockmaker, and in whose honour it was named. Admission is free though, since it is maintained by voluntary helpers, donations are always very welcome. There is a tea room for the thirsty.

Then, walking towards the High Street, you pass the *Coach House* and the *Place de Marines*. The *Coach House* once belonged to the *King's Head* and as you pass by look up inside for a moment at the roof timbers. Some of them have the 17th century assembly marks on them of the carpenters who made them and it has been suggested that this may have been the Market Hall which the celebrated Herefordshire carpenter John Abel built for the town in 1654.

Houses in the town being timber framed, despite their stone or brick frontages, fire was a major hazard. The hand-worked parish fire engine was kept in the churchyard, 6/8d a year being paid the unnamed individual who worked it. Then a fire brigade was formed in 1830. A new fire engine was acquired in 1859 and in 1888 the brigade became uniformed. A new horse-drawn Merryweather fire engine was purchased in 1893 and named the *Arrow*. By now the engine was kept here in Mill Street and the horses were pastured in the paddock of the *Burton Hotel*.

There was once a private house on the site of the *Burton Hotel* and the pig market was nearby. The hotel was built in 1851 and its assembly room was added in 1856. Several of the town's inns had such rooms for there was no public assembly room, though the assemblies were an important part of the social life of the more prosperous classes. The strictest etiquette was observed on these occasions and any breach thereof could have the most

9

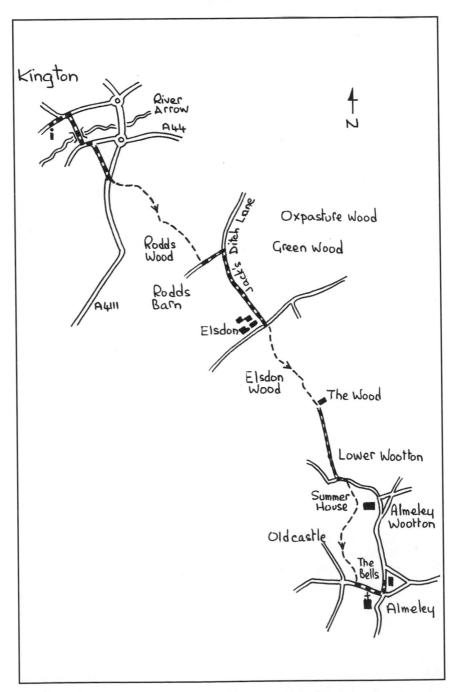

serious consequences. After such an assembly in 1808 Colonel John Walsham of Knill Court complained to Mr William Greenly of Titley Court 'when I bowed to you the other evening at the Kington Assembly, you hardly deigned to return the compliment. The reception I received from Mrs Greenly your wife was still more contemptuous and insulting.' Subsequently the 36 year old John Walsham challenged the 68 year old William Greenly to a duel with pistols. The outcome is unknown but such events were not unusual in early nineteenth century England.

It was here at the *Burton* that in October 1853 the town's railway career began in earnest when the first of a series of public meetings was held with the intention of 'having a Railway from Leominster to Kington, independent of any other line.' The line opened, after various vicissitudes, in 1857. The hotel was then known as *Milner's Family and Commercial Hotel*, after its proprietor John Meek Milner. He was enterprising enough when the railway opened to meet the trains at the station at the other end of the town with a horse drawn omnibus.

John Milner was also a wine and spirit merchant who for 'convenience of Private Consumers...imported in Quarter Casks, direct from the Vineyards...a choice selection of Fine Old Ports and Sherries of the first brands and of the most approved vintages'. This consideration, however, did not prevent his Assembly Room being rented in 1859 for Mr Onion's Temperance Meetings, attended apparently by some six hundred people, all no doubt drinking tea. Nowadays both afternoon tea and a choice of selection of fine old ports and sherries are still available at the Burton Hotel.

Next to the Burton stands the first building in the High Street, a four storey town house, with a neat three sided bay window on the ground floor. Stuccoed, it bears a plaque commemorating the fact that this junction of Mill Street, Church Street, and High Street, known as Upper Cross, was restored in 1879 and that JT Gwilliam was the builder who did the work. The house is now the premises of a beautician, and an adjacent archway gives access to *Harp Yard*. If you have the time, make a diversion into the yard, for it was here that in August 1746 that John Wesley preached:

> About ten we came to Kington, which they call eight miles from Leominster; I preached at one end of the town; the congregation divided itself into two parts, one half stood near, the other part remained a little way off, and lowr'd defiance, but the bridle from above was in their mouth, so they made no disturbance at all.

11

Regular Methodist services were established in the town in 1798 and after using various premises, in 1801 the Kington lawyer Edmund Cheese gave the congregation a small house in this yard to be converted into a chapel. It was enlarged in 1813 and in 1828 it was taken down and this much larger and grander chapel in stone under slate was built in the meeting house style. It served local needs until 1902 when a smaller, more ecclesiastical looking building replaced it on the corner of Churchill Road and Park Avenue. That in turn has also now gone and one of the houses standing on its site, is appropriately named *Ty Capel*, Chapel House. Now sadly dilapidated and long unused, the future of this once handsome chapel is the subject of considerable debate.

Opposite the Burton, Kington's Market Hall, though it is by no means the town's most treasured possession, has an interesting pedigree. In 1654 Philip Holman, Lord of the Manor of Huntington, of which Kington was part, lived in Bridge Street at Lyon House, now the *Talbot*. He commissioned John Abel the King's Carpenter, to erect a Market Hall on land behind his house, thereby giving the town, by using such an architect, a public building of some distinction. There was a measure of enlightened self-interest in this

Kington Market Hall

because, as Lord of the Manor, Holman was entitled to the market and fair day tolls.

This was not, however, the town's first Market Hall, for mention is made of one in a deposition of 1615, commemorated by Market Hall Street. Abel's Market Hall, lasted longer, surviving until 1820. It was replaced by a stone tiled successor, costing £500, to the design of Benjamin Wishlade, the town's best known architect. In 1841 the tiled roof of this Market House was replaced with slates by order of the then Lord of the Manor, John Thomas Woodhouse, of Leominster, an event which suggests though only 20 years old it was falling into disrepair. Its appearance is unknown but judging from Wishlade's designs for the National School and Court House and Police Station, it was stone built and functional in design, probably of one storey, the gabled roof being supported by open arches, linked by iron railings. The renovations to the roof ordered by John Woodhouse achieved little in the long run and eventually 'the roof fell in, and the ceiling, in rags, gave it a woeful appearance for many years, until it was replaced by cottages in 1876.'

It was felt, however, that the town should have a market hall and a more convenient site was sought. The centrally placed, but defunct *King's Head* at the Upper Cross was deemed ideal. The town's ratepayers in 1881 decided upon holding a public meeting at which it was resolved to build a new Market Hall on this site. The demolition of the *King's Head* began in January 1882. But it was not until December 1885 that the new Market Hall was opened and there was the inevitable small town controversy over the venture. A correspondent wrote to RW Banks, chairman of the Kington Improvement Commission, 'I suppose the rap is for you in the dear *Hereford Times* about the foolish Market House Scheme for Kington.'

This 'foolish market house' is the work of FR Kempson who also built the Anglican chapel of ease in Bridge Street and restored Huntington church. His work is ubiquitous in Herefordshire and the best known example is the City Library and Museum in Broad Street opposite Hereford cathedral.

The clock tower was added to the Market Hall to celebrate Queen Victoria's jubilee in 1897 and it has been suggested that iron work over the Market Hall entrances originated in Meredith's foundry at the other end of the town.

From the Market Hall we walk down the High Street on the left hand side of the road. Number 21, *Harts the Jewellers*, was built in the 17th century. It is timber framed and some of the carpenters' assembly marks have survived. There was a dummy run with houses such as these in the carpenter's yard and assembly marks were made to facilitate on-site erection. The overhanging upper floor, popular at this time to economise in space has often received the unwanted attentions of passing lorries. If you look up the drive way beside the shop you can see other timber framed buildings of the period.

Next door, number 20, *Clubsports*, in the nineteenth century was occupied by AH Wainwright, the Clothier and one is still reminded of the fact by his named being inscribed on the shop's mosaic door mat. This building also has some surviving vestiges of its original timber framing.

Further down, still using the left hand pavement, there is a bric-a-brac shop on the corner of Ellan Lane. It still has its attractive 19th century double shop front which in its day was the last word in mid-Victorian shop fitting. Rolled glass was introduced in the 1830s and the ornamental frieze running across the shop above the windows shows the kind of detail which is often now sacrificed as being incompatible with the image of modern marketing.

Still remaining on the left hand pavement cross over Prospect Lane and continue to number 13, *Sergeants*. The shop was built as an addition to a much older house behind it which is thought to date back to the 14th century. Its antiquity is reflected by its being of cruck construction. Four pairs of massive crucks were used with a span of some 21 feet and this has led to the suggestion that the building originally had some civic or craft guild function when New Kington was developing at the bottom of the hill whereon the castle and the parish church were the nucleus of the original Old Kington.

It was here at number 13 that in 1866 AW Gamage and his sister opened their doors as drapers. His window, devoted to headgear was deemed to be 'the brightest spot in town, and his two or three lady assistants were very attractive...the lovely hats must have made many women weep in their desire for them.' But Mr Gamage had gone to London by 1881 where he set up his famous store in High Holborn.

It is time now to look back up the High Street at the opposite side which is best seen without crossing the road. Things, at least architecturally, are seldom what they seem in Kington. Thus number 33, *Thirty-Three,* a newsagents, has all the appearance with its sash windows of an early Victorian structure. But within there are beams enriched with mouldings which witness to the 17th century origins of the building. Buildings were seldom pulled down, instead the parts which could be seen were revamped according to the fashions of the time. What could not be seen was left alone.

Next to *Thirty Three*, is *Bopsam and Son, Nightingales,* and then number 36, *The Chocolate Box.* This is another survivor from the timber framed period and the complexity of its architectural history can be seen by glancing up the lane beside it.

Then past *The Wine Vaults* we come to a large frontage occupied by a grocery shop, *Right Price*. At the turn of the century Francis Parker and Son, General Drapers occupied the shop and their mosaic door mat survives at the entrance [as opposed to the exit]. The whole building was refronted in the late eighteenth century, though some of the original timber framing survives at the rear. Its sash windows, gable pediment, and pilasters made it one of the most prosperous looking establishments of its day.

Look past *Glyn Slade Jones*, the butchers, to number 40, *Hair Port*. Here the mosaic doormat tells us that these were once the premises of Thomas Hall and Sons, grocers. A photograph taken c. 1900 shows how labour intensive these shops were and a staff of ten are posing for the photographer. Mr Hall himelf prospered and lived at Castle Hill House.

Now beyond an alley way, past *Hodges, Dawsons the Chemists, Peacehaven,* and the exotically named *Mi-Mi la Sardine*, to number 45, *Alpha Antiques*. It was here that Thomas Skarratt, 1776-1838, the clock maker had his home and shop, and his eldest son Henry, 1809-1888, a watch maker, after him. In 1841 Henry Skarratt placed a clock in the shop window which was lit by gas at night for the convenience of any member of the public wanting to know the time. It was, however, Skarratt time and those travelling by the *Mazeppa* stage coach were warned on the time timetable:

> Notice! This starts from the Oxford Arms, Kington every Tuesday, Thursday, and Saturday Morning, quarter before Seven o'Clock, London Time and not by Skarratt's Clock.

In December 1853 the railway arrived at Hereford and with its coming Herefordshire lost eleven minutes, never to be regained, for, to enable the trains to run to schedule, London time finally supplanted its counterparts like that of Mr Skarratt.

Then look past *Jane's Parlour*, with more rolled glass, beyond a former green grocery shop, and a florists, to number 49-50, the butcher's shop of *Paul Lewis*. Again, it looks as if it were built in the eighteenth century and it was certainly at that time it acquired its first floor Venetian window. But an interior ceiling was discovered to conceal beams belonging to the late 16th or early 17th centuries. So once again we can see how the public face of Kington was totally transformed in the eighteenth century when all the timber framed buildings in its two main streets were given rubble frontages concealed with roughcast covering.

It is time now to continue our walk down the High Street, still on the left hand pavement. Pass number 9, the *White Swan Steak Bar,* which within has a wealth of interesting woodwork showing its age, like many other buildings in the High Street, is far greater than is implied by the frontage. Continue to *Barclays Bank* and before considering the bank itself, look across the road at what used to be known as the *Chained Swan.* It shows how, in the town's eighteenth century rebuild, the inns were the trend setters. The *Chained Swan* displays many of the architectural conceits of its day, and still has its moulded swan inn sign. JW Tonkin, the Herefordshire doyen of architectural historians, asked whether its predecessor was the *Fox and Swan* of 1707. If so, the building before us underwent a considerable degree of upward social mobility. For in 1707 it was kept by a widow and consisted of twelve rooms; downstairs there was a kitchen, cellar, buttery, brew house, a little parlour with a room adjoining. Upstairs there was a cheese chamber, a room at the stairs head, two rooms known as the *Fox and Swan,* the best chamber, and the chamber next the fold. A century later it was of three storeys, had acquired a classical frontage with Venetian windows on the first floor, an enriched pediment and pilasters, and an assembly room had been built at the rear.

It closed as an inn in 1842 and it is now occupied by three shops and it has lost some of its original good looks. Number 51, *Morgans,* became the shop of Charles Humphreys, bookseller, stationer, and printer. It was he who, in 1845, printed Richard Parry's *History of Kington.* He also published a weekly newspaper, The *Kington Gazette & Radnorshire Chronicle,* which first appeared in September 1862 and cost one penny for four pages. It is said to have had a weekly circulation of a hundred copies. It was here, too, that the Mechanics Institute, founded in 1841, met. During its short life it provided its members with lectures, a library, reading room, and a museum.

But now turn your back on the *Chained Swan* to consider the premises of *Barclays Bank.* It was once the shop of Merediths the ironmongers and the proprietors of the Kington Foundry. Their name can still be seen over the door, and the rolled glass windows and the high quality of the decoration of this shop front underline its nineteenth century primacy in the High Street. Other activities went on here besides the sale of ironmongery and at one stage it was advertised that

> the Misses Meredith receive a limited number of pupils to educate on modern principles. Physical culture a speciality.

It is part, you will see, of a much larger building, which is considered to be the best piece of public architecture of the Kington architect and

Radnorshire County Surveyor, Benjamin Wishlade, 1768-1848, who lived in Duke Street. To see it at its best, cross the High Street to the other side.

Built in 1845 in the classical style, Pevsner described it as having 'a five bay centre with lower wings, all with giant pilasters, and with a cornice decorated with pretty wreaths.' Sadly, the interior arrangements of Wishlade's Town Hall were quite unsuitable for municipal use, but an enlightened District Council restored and rebuilt it in 1977, and converted the upper floors into flats. It is now recovering from a recent fire.

Next to the bank and sharing Wishlade's building is the town's bow fronted computer centre, KC3. The town's Literary Institute was once housed here. Next door to the Town Hall is the rather earlier and rather demure building of the Midland Bank. A plaque on the wall tells you that it was here that the highly successful Kington and Radnorshire Bank was founded in 1808. James Watt was one of its customers. It acquired its pair of bow windows in 1873, whereas those of the computer centre are modern reproductions. In 1910 the Bank was bought by the Metropolitan Bank for £29,500, which, in turn, became part of the Midland Bank.

Traffic jams are a familiar sight in the High Street despite the relief offered by the opening of the by-pass in March 1983. The turn into Bridge Street is particularly vulnerable, but it has always been so, and in 1866 the manager of the Kington and Radnorshire Bank was alarmed when 'a large elm tree nearly went into the Bank window in turning the corner. The horses were unhooked and the tree was sawn through before they could proceed.' Traffic permitting, once past the bank, turn right now into Bridge Street. On the left hand corner stands the *Public Library*. It was not until 1927 that Kington acquired a public library though the first Public Libraries Act was passed in 1850. Its present premises, once shared with the *Arrow Lodge* of Freemasons, were originally the registered offices of the *Old Radnor Trading Company*, founded in 1875. It was built in 1905, an event marked by a dated drainpipe, on this prestigious corner site, made available by the demolition of the *Old Harp* Inn. You will notice that the building has been recessed by two feet this side and by one foot on the Duke Street side. This is held to be an early example of town planning, the revised building line being insisted upon to widen the very narrow pavement somewhat. The *Kington Past* Plaque on the Library wall is worth reading.

Next to the *Library* comes the *Post Office*. Rebuilt in recent times, its ground floor discreetly art nouveau character, achieved with ornamental yellow bricks and leaded glass, has been preserved.

On the opposite corner is the *Corner Shop* of Rose Davies and *Albion House*, once the *Albion Hotel*, is next door. The *Corner Shop* with its puny exposed timbers shows that errors of judgement in the treatment of buildings are not just a contemporary characteristic. Happily, *Albion House*, shows how it was intended both buildings should appear when they were built at the end of the eighteenth century. The timbers were meant to be covered and look much better for being so. Note *Albion House's* rich pediment with its gothick round-topped sash window.

Next door, number 3, *King's News* has retained its original bow windows. Colour washed brick has been used for this house of three stories. Brick was introduced for its convenience as a building material and for its fire resistant properties. The decorated cornice beneath the guttering gives the building an air of prosperity.

Number 4 and number 5 share three gables, one of which still has its medieval timbers exposed. The equally ancient interior roof timbers have also survived and the whole structure stands in contrast to the later buildings on either side.

Number 6, the *Angel Fish and Chip shop*, has a wooden first floor balcony with shaped balusters. There was a short-lived taste in the town for this kind of decoration and there are some late eighteenth century shops with similar balconies in Church Street and on the former *Oxford Arms* in Duke Street. Number 7 is very similar, though lacking a balcony. It is such a pity that a far from beautiful lamp post has had to be so clumsily placed in front of it.

On the same side as we are walking, on the left hand pavement, we come to the *Baptist Chapel*. The town's original Baptist chapel was erected in 1810 and enlarged in 1821. The present building in the fashionable temple style, with pilasters and pediment, which was favoured when nonconformists were anxious not to be accused of aping Anglican gothic, was erected in 1869. An insensitively placed telephone box obscures the quiet dignity of its facade. The limited financial resources available only allowed the transformation to be applied to the chapel's frontage and the sides and back are much simpler in style.

Numbers 55 and 54 next below the chapel are brick built and have retained their original 19th century multi-paned shop windows though they are now both private houses.

Opposite on the other side of the road, an alleyway between numbers 7 and 8 gives access to a cottage built on Number 7's burgage plot. This reflects a temporary growth of pressure on building plots which resulted in a limited measure of seventeenth and eighteenth century in-filling. Nineteenth century expansion was suburban, on the outskirts of the town, as was the case with Victoria Road, the continuation of Duke Street.

Number 8, the *Opticians*, is another late 18th or early 19th century house, and has a rather small pair of bay windows either side of the doorway which is supported by decoratively reeded pilasters. Several of the houses in Bridge Street have modestly ceremonial doorways, the dignity of which have been enhanced in these two houses by being set at the head of a small flight of stone steps, reflecting Georgian taste and the social custom of the formal visiting. This kind of doorway was not intended to encourage casual dropping in, but for the reception of those being received when the mistress of the house was *At Home*. The wide eaves of this house are often characteristic of late 18th or early 19th century buildings. Number 9, next door, is another house with a handsome formal doorway.

Continuing down the left hand side of Bridge Street we come now to the *Talbot*. Do not be put off by its rather unpromising Victorianised frontage. In the early 17th century this was the home of the Lord of the Manor and called *Lyon House*. The original frontage of the house looked sideways on to Market Hall Street and it is from here we can imagine its original appearance. An addition was made in the eighteenth century at the Bridge Street end, which later lost its overall Georgian appearance by the addition in the late nineteenth century of a disproportionately large and sashed bow window. At the gable end of this extension, looking into Market Hall Street, it would seem that four windows have been blocked to avoid window tax.

Inside, its handsome Jacobean circular wooden staircase has been recently restored and some other original woodwork has survived which maybe even earlier. Cross Market Hall Street, sparing a more than a passing glance at number 12 on the opposite side of Bridge Street. Here is another good doorway, its eliptical fanlight being almost reminiscent of Dublin. This house and its neighbour number 11 were originally one and were converted into two in 1778. Previously, it had been the *Tennice Court*, where the tennis played was, of course real Real Tennis, rather than lawn tennis.

Further down on the same side, number 16 has its original leaded glass in its gable window and its neighbour, number 17, has a nice leaded Venetian window in its gable. Then comes number 18, again, it is much older than it looks, and stretches back into its burgage plot in a variety of architectural styles. It was here that the lawyer Richard Banks made his home when he came to Kington in 1814 and founded the branch of the Banks family which still flourishes in the town.

Back on the left hand side of the road continue past the *Queen's Head*, noticing the reeded pillasters all along the ground floor, and the exposed timber framing of its side wing. Beyond the *Queen's Head* comes number 47, a three storey town house, with a cellar and a stuccoed frontage concealing the rubble walls behind it. Lines have been drawn on the stucco to give the impression that it is really built in ashlar, which was far more costly. There are two small ground floor bays with sash windows and larger sash windows on the first floor. The attics, for the servants, are lit by small casement windows. Next onto the *Kingdom Hall of Jehovah's Witnesses*. This small chapel was erected in 1859 for the town's Primitive Methodists but between the wars it enjoyed an episode as the Kington Cinema.

Now continue on the left hand pavement to the third ecclesiastical building in Bridge Street. This is the *Roman Catholic Church of St Bede*. It was designed by FR Kempson, 1837-1923, as an Anglican chapel of ease. He also designed the Market Hall and restored Huntington church.

Next comes the *Telephone Exchange*, surely Kington's plainest and most unimaginative piece of architecture. It shares these premises with *KC3*.

Finally, on the right hand side of the road, there is an example of early 20th century industrial architecture. Once a garage, and then a tyre depot, it now awaits a new role. This was the site of the timber framed *Porch House* which derived its name from its two storey porch. It was moved, lock, stock, and barrel, to Church Bank in the 1930s. It was one of the status houses which made Lower Kington the place to live in the 16th and 17th centuries.

If you have time and interest, once past the old tyre depot, turn right to gain access to the *Turner's Mill* complex. Looking through the gates you will see the mill and its attendant granary before you and the miller's house, *Arrow Lodge*, on your right. It reflects his prosperity in Georgian times, with its fashionable lunette in its pediment. He only altered the front, however, which was later Victorianized, giving the house a certain heaviness of appearance, which would look right in a northern mill town like Huddersfield. The rest of the house was left untouched, but when the Victorian refurbishing took place, his successor took the opportunity of having the two cottages opposite the stream, *Island Cottages*, up-dated as well, raising their height and giving them a new front in dressed stone and with sash windows. At the back the original casement windows and rubble walls can be seen and one concludes that middle class life in Kington was very competitive.

Resuming our walk, continue over the bridge. The Arrow would originally have been crossed by a ford, until a wooden bridge replaced it, which, in turn, gave way to a stone successor. It may have been this bridge which suffered in the great storm of February 1795 when the Arrow rose ten feet at Kington. This bridge was replaced in 1810 having become ruinous and the new structure in stone was carried on four arches and with its cut-waters would have been a handsome addition to the town's architecture. It was drastically rebuilt and widened in the last century between the wars.

Old Bridge House, was once an inn, the *Bridge End*, and is much older than its brick front and modern windows would suggest. Then comes the refurbished toll house on the corner of Kingswood Road. This was once the main road to Hereford. The opposite corner is occupied by a colour washed cottage with its original stone tiled roof. The timber-framed gable facing Kingswood Road has been filled in with bricks, replacing the original wattle and daub.

But remaining with the main road, on the right hand side the massive form of *Perseverance Works*, its ground floor of whitewashed brick, with timber upper storeys, dominates the scene. It was once a granary and still has its owl holes for the convenience of the visits of these hunters of the mice and rats which fed on the grain. In 1876 it was the premises of Richard Roberts, a builder and builders' merchant. Roberts, a native of Pembridge, lived on the premises with his wife and six children, and advertized his ability to supply 'plans, specifications, and estimates, and his stock of all kinds of building materials, including English and Foreign timber and seasoned boards'. The use of the name *Perseverance* reflects the Victorian values represented by the building. Tradition has it that at one stage it was a hostel for migrant workers who came into the town to help with the harvest. It also had a period as a carriage works and then later it became a garage. It is now a furniture factory specializing in making quality reproductions.

Beyond the *Perseverance* building and *Perseverance Close,* a small cluster of modern houses, comes *Lomas's Total Garage.* Avert your gaze from here to the buildings opposite which are far more interesting. There is a terrace of three small late nineteenth century brick built cottages, with wood framed casements. Then an older, more substantial stone built and colour washed cottage with attractive sash windows. The group is completed by a pair of much more modern white-washed brick cottages with *Philpots Hairdressing Salon* finishing the range. All in all it is a commentary on the evolution of small town working class domestic architecture from 1750 to 1900.

21

Pass the garage and then turn right up a road which proclaims it is not a thoroughfare for motorists, though it was once the main road to Eardisley. Cross *Banley Drive* on the left with its cluster of newly built houses in brick, and pass a selection of post war houses, representing Kington's suburbia, complete with laurels and conifers. These give way to the twenty-first century with open plan front gardens. The entrance to *Banley Farm* is on the right and ahead the road becomes a footpath, complete with its own finger board. We are now out into the open country. The footpath's career is short-lived, and, on arriving at a road blocking one's way, follow the advice of the directing arrow, and turn left.

Cross the present Eardisley road, and following the signpost enter the field by crossing the stile to the left of the iron gate. Once in the field carry on across it, making for the first electricity pylon. Continue on, the ground gently rising, and aim for the oak trees ahead. Arriving at a stile, cross it and follow the direction of the arrow, turning to your left and following the hedge. Though Gabby was on the lead, the sheep were alarmed to see us: the first members of the outside world they had seen, we suppose, for six months or more. Quite soon there is another stile on the right. Cross over it using the little bridge which is part of its structure. Following the direction of the arrow ahead, ignoring the gap to the left, and go straight on with the fence and hedge on your left. Looking back, the town of Kington stretches out before you and the valley beyond, leading into Wales. *Ridgebourne*, prim and neat, with its double gables, can be seen above Kington, presiding over the town's affairs, as it has for nearly two hundred years. It is the home of the Banks family: Richard Banks, a young lawyer from Kent, settled in Kington in 1814 and five generations of the family have served the town as lawyers, bankers, scholars, and benefactors.

Arriving at an iron gate, use the stile on the left, and continue by following the margin of the field on your left. The going can now be quite difficult because there is a ditch immediately to the left of your path waiting for you to fall in. Carry on until you bear left at a corner, the fence is to the left enclosing a row of mature trees. Continue until you arrive at another gate, which is ignored, and instead bear right and follow the hedge. Cross a dilapidated stile to your left. Once over it, turn right, and lying on the ground there is an orange arrow, pointing more or less in the right direction. When there were crops growing in the field, rather than cause damage, it is tempting to walk around the margin, instead of following strictly the route of the public footpath. However, for legal reasons, do not do this and always keep strictly to the path.

Looking to your right, over the hedge and beyond, you will see the cemetery on the far side of the Kington-Eardisley road. The opening of a public cemetery on the outskirts of the town in 1862 meant nonconformists no longer had to be buried in the already overcrowded Anglican churchyard. The cemetery was the first fruits of the town's Burial Board set up in 1859 in consequence of the Burial Act of 1852. The land was bought at 150 guineas per acre from Sir Harford Brydges of Boultibrooke near Presteign. It was deemed to be 'the prettiest site and the nearest to the town which the Board could obtain', but Sir George Cornewall Lewis, MP for New Radnor and Secretary of State for the War Department, was told it was 'unnecessarily large and expensive and so distant from the town as to be inconvenient.'

Choosing the site involved a degree of Victorian Nimbyism. RW Banks of Ridgebourne was the chairman of the Burial Board and, after complaining about the time that it took to inspect the various sites, expressed his satisfaction that the site chosen 'relieves us from all fear of a cemetery near Ridgebourne, which might have happened.' Three years later the vicar told him 'that the Chapels at the Cemetery are almost finished and that the interior arrangements are very good, as well as the glazing, which is done by plumbers from Birmingham.' Built in stone under slate there were two chapels, serving the needs of Protestants and Roman Catholics, and a keeper's cottage.

Through a fair degree of Victorian nepotism, the choice of architect fell upon Edward Haycock, junior, b. 1830, an architect from Shrewsbury, and son of the county surveyor of Shropshire. It so happened that Haycock was married to Georgiana Miles, of Dunfield, near Kington, and his father-in-law, Henry Miles, JP, and High Sheriff of Radnorshire in 1847 very kindly paid his son-in-law's £50 fee for the plans.

But to return to the walk. There are more mature trees on the right to shade the way as one follows the margin of the field. Our route is now climbing steadily. Follow the direction of the arrow to the corner of the field and cross a stile into another field, leaving the trees behind us. The arrow on the stile directs our course straight ahead. Gabby, of course, had to be carried over these frequent stiles, too high to be jumped, an indignity she eventually took with resignation.

Now with the fence to our left, again with a row of handsome mature oaks giving it extra definition, the field itself was occupied by sheep and the going was easier, with no growing crops to avoid. In the corner of the field, still following up the left side, there is a stile to be crossed. This next field when we came to it had been a meadow and the hay had been cut. Cross the field to a stile amongst a row of trees, and the reassuring sign of the arrow. Over the stile, look back over the fine view towards Wales, before going on through a wood of mature trees, *Rodds Wood*. There is also *Rodds Farm* in the vicinity and the *Rodd* element shared by all these names is derived from the Old English *rod*, denoting a clearing, once again reflecting the well-wooded nature of the terrain in former times.

It was many months since this path through *Rodds Wood* was last walked and there were many welcoming brambles and nettles to greet us on our way. The going is now gently downhill. When we arrived at a grassy track, instead of crossing it, and stumbling further through the wood, which had acquired something of the character of an Amazonian forest, we turned right down the track for a short way and were rewarded by a fine display of ferns and wild flowers. One soon arrives at a T-junction and a proper farm track, leading from *Rodds Barn*. Here we turned left, coming soon to stiles opposite each other to our left and right. We would have come over the left-hand stile had we persevered through the wood where the going was difficult.

We should then have crossed the farm track over the right hand stile. However, we couldn't get Gabby over the stile, it was too high, so we continued along the farm track instead, and arriving soon at a T-junction we turned right into the intriguingly named *Jack's Ditch Lane*. The identity of Jack who long ago drained the lane with a ditch has long been lost, but one is grateful for what he did. Wooded on both sides, *Green Wood* and *Oxpasture Wood* beyond tell their own story about the landscape. For centuries the ox was preferred to the horse for drawing the plough. Though slower and more cumbersome than the horse, the ox was stronger and had more stamina. It was also easier to keep, less likely to become ill, and there was bonus that at then end of its working life it could be fattened up and sold as meat.

So, continuing down *Jack's Ditch Lane*, one comes to the iron gate with a footpath sign on the right hand side, which we would have used had we been able to get ourselves over the stile in the track from *Rodds Barn*. Opposite this and a little before *Green Cottages* on the other side of the lane, a finger post on a stile directs one diagonally to the right across what was on the day of our walk a ploughed field. Just before the stile in this field there was a horseshoe in the ploughed earth, as if a ploughing team had passed that way and one of the horses had cast its shoes. But, of course, that was no more than a romantic reminiscence.

Progress over the stile was obstructed by a herd of Limousin bullocks. They looked very pretty, but we felt disinclined to insist upon our right to cross the field by that particular route. So instead, we turned right and followed the margin of the field, back tracking briefly, to *Jack's Ditch Lane*. Turning left into the lane we went on our way. A few vehicles did pass us, so some caution is required here. The farm, which is now to the left, bears the historic name *Elsdon*. This occurs in 1086 in Domesday as the name of the Hundred. Counties were once divided into hundreds for administrative reasons and the place-name Hundred House commemorates where the business of the hundred was discussed.

Originally a possession of the de Lacys, *Elsdon* belonged to the Pember family of Newport, Almeley until the middle of the eighteenth century. Francis Pember was a 17th century benefactor of Lady Hawkins' School, founded in 1632 in Kington, and the family were generally prominent in local affairs.

Coming now to a T-junction we cross the Bollingham-Lyonshall unclassified road, where a stile awaits us. Over the stile and follow the direction of the finger post to walk diagonally to your right over the field of pasture. Descend the hill, past the large tree-shaded pond, which is on your left, and join the cart track, which has also descended from *Elsdon*. The track leads to a securely tied gate, through which the arrow bids us pass. So patiently untying and retying both sets of knots, the owner being decidely opposed to our walking in this direction, we went on our way, past *Elsdon Wood*, which is to our right.

Now we go through a gateless pair of gateposts across a field diagonally to the right. Ahead is a farm called *The Wood*. Having crossed the field follow the yellow arrow and bear to the right along the margin of the field. On arriving at stile to your left, despite its rather overgrown access, cross it. Pass through a small field being used as a dump for waste, corrugated iron and wood barns on your left.

Then, as you join the lane giving access to *The Wood*, turn right. The hedges on either side are rich in blackberry brambles, wild roses, honeysuckle, ferns, and wild flowers. Half a mile on we arrive at *Lower Wootton*. The name is derived from the Old English *Wudu-tun*, and commemorates *the farmstead or settlement in or by the wood*. The old farmhouse, on the left hand side of the lane, and set back, is large and timber framed. With hipped gables and a large stone chimney, it is L-shaped and was built early in the seventeenth century. Later a partial third story was added.

Ignoring the finger post telling us of a path to the right, continue on down the lane. And on the right hand side you will soon come to a stile, with arrow and finger post. The actual stile is heavily disguised by brambles, but to Gabby's delight, on examination, it proved to be a de-luxe model, with a dog gate. Follow the direction of the finger post and walk diagonally to the left across the pasture. Aim for the oak in crossing the field, and another luxury stile awaits you. Turn right, and a hundred yards ahead another stile, complete with guiding arrow, confronts you. The path now descends quite steeply and there is handrail for one's safety. One arrives at another T-junction with a guiding three directional finger post.

We turned to the right, but the antiquarians amongst us might want to turn left where a very short diversion will take you to the seventeenth century *Summer House*. Volume III of the Royal Commission on Historical Monuments England's *Inventory of the Historical Monuments in Herefordshire*, describes the building in some detail. It was once occupied by the Almeley Quaker, Roger Prichard, who died in 1679, and whose initials are painted on one of the gable lozenges. It was he, who in 1672 gave the timber framed and hipped-roofed cottage for use as a Quaker meeting house at nearby Almeley Wootton. Set in its own graveyard, where all the tomb stones are of uniformly modest design and size, it is on the left hand side of the road from Almeley to Lyonshall, but is easily accessible from the *Summer House*. Why the name *Summer House*? Is this a relic from the days of transhumance commemorated in Wales by the place-names *Hafod* and *Hendre*, for the summer and winter residences?

But to return to our walk, which took us down a pleasant wooded farm lane, past *Fir Tree Cottage* on your right. A little footbridge will take you across the stream if so wish, but another arrow suggests that we continue on our chosen path which is well wooded, with a stream flowing below us to the left. This stream, which eventually makes its way, via the so-called Letton Lake to the Wye a little above Bredwardine, was probably important to the development of Almeley. It provided earlier inhabitants with a water supply, power to work their mill, and something of a moat for the protection of Old Castle, the site of which rises up above the trees to our right. The path was very muddy and when a finger post offered us an alternative by turning to the left, we took it. A handrail protects one from a sudden descent into the stream below and still in the woods we cross the stream first by a wooden footbridge and then a little later by one of concrete. There is a kissing gate in front of us, asking those going in the opposite direction to keep their dogs on a lead. Soon an arrow will offer the alternative of a sharp turn to the left: take this offer up, the path goes back upon itself whilst climbing up the side of the valley and along here we turned right again. After some steps comes a stile with a dog gate, and a finger post tells us our path takes us across a meadow. There are fine views of the Welsh hills to our right. Leaving the meadow by a gate, well secured by twine on the day of our walk, we come into suburban Almeley. Leave *Ashcroft* at a T-junction by turning right into *Mountain View*, with the back of a row of council houses to your left and the *Old Coach House* on your right. Go on to Manor Close, which leads into the main road. Turn right, and past the *Old Vicarage,* the *Bells* await your arrival, with appropriate hospitality, on the other side of the road.

The Bells is on the left, side ways on, two storeys, stone, long and low. In 1852 it was conducted by John Morris, who doubled as a blacksmith. He was succeeded by Thomas Holland, who advertised himself in 1874 as a builder and contractor. The hospitality offered by *The Bells* was augmented by the *New Inn*, where William Vaughan, the landlord, would make you a pair of boots or shoes, as well as supply you with beer. Stephen John, of the *Queen's Head* at Woonton offered a similar service, whereas Ann Hall, of *The Buck Inn* at Woonton, stuck to her last, as it were, and was happy to describe herself simply as a victualler. In 1853 Henry Baird of Almeley set himself up as a wholesale and family brewer, 'supplying Families and the Trade with Genuine Home Brewed Ales, Brewed purely with Malt and Hops, guaranteed free from the slightest adulteration, or deleterious ingredient of any description'. Moreover, he could supply his wares 'in casks from 9 to 54 gallons'. Perhaps they were supplied by Thomas Lloyd, the Woonton cooper and shop keeper, the malt coming from John Owen, of the *Meer*, farmer and malster.

In 1852 the village was largely self-contained, there were twenty farmers, some of whom were also cattle dealers, whose needs were supplied by several shopkeepers and bootmakers, a tailor, a carpenter and joiner, a wheelright, and a horsebreaker. There was also a schoolmaster and schoolmistress, sexton and parish clerk, a parson, and a squire.

WALKING WITH A GREYHOUND

ALMELEY

Almeley is another of the many Herefordshire place-names commemo-rating the county's once well-wooded character. It appears in Domesday as *Elmelie* and is derived from the Old English *elmleah*, 'an elm wood'. But by then sufficient numbers of the elms had been cleared to pro-vide arable land to occupy the labour of eight ploughs; indeed there was work enough to employ as well 'the men of another village', identified as neighbouring *Upcot*.

Also according to Domesday Almeley was part of the endowments of the pre-Norman priory of St Guthlac in Hereford before passing into the hands of Roger de Lacy whose extensive estates in Herefordshire were centred upon Weobley. Roger, the son of Walter de Lacy who died in 1085, played an important part in the defence of the English frontier against the Welsh. His loyalties, however, were uncertain and he rebelled unsuccessfully against William Rufus in 1088 and 1094, and was banished. His lands were given to his brother Hugh. Roger died sometime after 1106 in Normandy where he attained high office under Robert, Duke of Normandy and William the Conqueror's eldest son.

As part of the de Lacys' defensive strategy there were two castles at Almeley. The site of the smaller and probably the older of the two, *Oldcastle Twt*, is north west of the village and we passed it on our way. There is an irony in using the Welsh adjective *twt*, small, neat, to describe this castle, for its pur-pose was to keep the Welsh at bay. But in the twelfth century Welsh was to be heard in Almeley, well within *Herefordia in Wallia* as defined by the line of Offa's Dyke. The village commands fine views of the Welsh border which reminded many of its inhabitants of their roots. *Oldcastle Twt* has a circular motte, some 29ft in diameter at the top, 18ft or so above the ditch below, and is thought by Raven, though 'overgrown', still to be 'impressive'. A rectan-gular bailey stands to the north. Later, a larger castle was built, south west of the parish church. It has a circular motte 36ft or so in diameter at its top, about 21ft above the bottom of the ditch below, and is set on the south side of a quadrangular bailey. The churchyard has encroached upon the filled-in ditch on the north-east side of the bailey.

29

To the south-west of the castle there were fish ponds, essential for the provision of its Lenten and Friday fare. Salter points out that the castle would have been difficult to defend after the nearby parish church acquired a tower c.1200. However, it remained functional to some extent, and William Cantelupe, d.1239, one of King John's 'evil counsellors', was its constable in 1216, the year of the latter's death. In 1242 Henry III, 1216-72, received the homage here of Simon de Montfort. The estate was occupied by Roger Pychard 1242, a member of the knightly family commemorated by the Herefordshire place name Ocle Pychard.

In 1863 the Cambrian Archaeological Association visited Almeley parish church, and pronounced it to be:

> a rare specimen of a large country church of the fourteenth century, in excellent preservation, and not yet mutilated or disfigured by restorers. It was universally allowed to be the most interesting church, with the exception of that of Moccas, of all the buildings visited by them during the meeting.

That was before its restoration in 1868. After this the omniscient nineteenth century vicar of Norton Canon, the Revd Charles J Robinson, writing in 1872, considered Almeley parish church to be one of the finest in the diocese, noting, perhaps to reassure the Cambrians, that it had 'lately been restored with great taste and judgement'. This tasteful restoration cost £1,800 and was no doubt due to the initiative of the aristocratically named vicar, the Revd William Pitcairn Alexander Campbell, MA, of Queen's College, Cambridge. He was instituted in 1865 and remained at Almeley until 1877,when he received the due reward for his pastoral industry. The Bishop of Worcester, patron of the living of Almeley, worth a mere £254 per annum, presented him to another of the livings in his gift, that of Fladbury near Evesham, worth £780. Campbell had eight children, so no doubt needed the extra stipend.

Enter its well kept churchyard by the attractive double iron gates given in 1997. Almeley parish church is one of the 2,335 ancient churches dedicated to Our Lady, the most popular dedication in the country. It was particularly popular with the Normans who frequently established churches in her honour alongside their castles, as can be seen locally at Kington, Pembridge, and Almeley. They did this because they saw the parish church as much as the castle as being a means of conquest and subjugation.

Nothing of this original Norman church has survived and the lower part of the early 13th century tower is the oldest part of the building. This tower, in military fashion, is battered, with no external entrance, and may have played a defensive role or at least have been built by those who built the castles. The church was rebuilt later that century, and given a spacious chancel to accommodate the growing liturgical requirements of the day. The arched recess, on the north side of the chancel, was once deeper than it is at present, and may have accommodated an effigy. The Cambrians, the ecclesiological experts of their day, thought 'the *piscina* on the south side is a good specimen, while the *sedilia* have been cleverly cut out of the window-sill'. The piscina was a stone basin with a drain, used for washing the communion vessels at then end of the liturgy, and the sedilia was a set of three seats for the comfort of the clergy during the readings of the day, or when when the mass had prolonged musical interludes.

Later a chantry chapel, with a room above for the accommodation of the celibate priest, was added to the south side of the chancel. It is now a vestry. There were further additions in the fourteenth century in the form of aisles to the north and south of nave, each with a side chapel at their east ends. These and the east window of the chancel have rich tracery in the style of the decorated period. These extensions necessitated raising the roof level of the nave and providing it with clerestorys. The Cambrians with a commendable lack of affectation, long since abandoned by architectural historians, spoke of 'the clearstory windows', noting with approval that they were large, and contained 'good decorated tracery'.

When these clerestories were added, it seems that the very large stones which were used, in contrast to small stones of the chancel, were recycled from the decaying castle nearby. All the roofs have been fortunate enough to retain their stone tiles. Externally, however, the visual effect of the church is not entirely satisfactory because the main mass of nave, aisles, and chancel is disproportionately large to sit comfortably with the older tower, which belonged to a smaller building.

Refreshing, simple modern glass fills the small lancet window in the porch, and when we came on a hot summer's day, the ancient door was open in welcome. Within one was immediately struck that we were entering the church of a lively worshipping community, not an antiquarian repository.

In a medieval church the carved wooden screens promoted a sense of reverence and mystery. This was particularly so with the rood screen separating chancel from nave, with a representation above the screen of Christ on his cross and with St Mary and St John standing on either side. A staircase, set into the north side of the chancel arch gained access to the rood loft above the screen. The ceiling above the present rood screen, painted as it is in yellow, blue, black and red to imitate square moulded panels with bosses and Tudor roses, reminds one of the overall richness of a medieval church. The symbolic roses remind us there was little distinction between politics and religion in the early sixteenth century and that Henry VIII was Defender of the Faith, a title bestowed upon him by the Pope and still enjoyed by the Queen, and Supreme Governor of the English Church. It is likely that this canopy of honour over the rood once extended into to the chancel itself, or at least had a counterpart over the sanctuary.

The Reformation saw the rood altar and the representation of crucifixion dismantled, and a singing loft took its place. The tower, on the other hand, gained a screen, removed from elsewhere in the church. This new Jacobean screen defined the space for a school and some benches belong to the same period, for pews were a new fashion, and the sermons of the reformed clergy very long. To accommodate the restored practice of the congregation receiving the chalice at holy communion, a silver chalice and paten was acquired from a London silver smith in 1613. The keeping of parish registers, recording baptisms, marriages, and burials became compulsory in 1538 and the earliest survivor of Almeley's registers is dated 1595.

The tower houses a clock and six bells, rung from the ground floor. Their predecessors were destroyed when the tower was struck and badly damaged by lightning in 1518.The present bell frame is supported on four huge oak posts, which reach right down to the ground, one in each corner of the tower. Thomas Rudhall, whose famous bell foundry was at Gloucester, cast three of the bells in 1773. Founded by his great grandfather, Abraham Rudhall, in the period 1684-1830 some 4,500 bells were cast at Gloucester, including those of several London churches. Another bell was acquired in 1866, from the London firm of bell founders, Mears and Stainbank who can number Big Ben as one of their more famous castings. They also supplied the treble bell in 1930 in memory of Cecilia Teresa Hunt. The sixth bell, weighing 11 hundred weights, was commissioned in 1960 from another famous foundry, that of John Taylor of Loughborough, and bears the legend often inscribed on bells: 'I to church the living call, I to the grave summon all'. Taylors also renewed all the bell fittings of the tower. Besides summoning parishioners to worship, the bells have been rung over the centuries to commemorate both parochial and national events. Bell ringing is a strenuous occupation and the ringers often refreshed themselves afterwards in the nearby inn, and so for that matter did churchwardens, the entry 'ale for my trouble' occurring frequently in their accounts. A village also took pride in its bells, so that they are often mentioned on inn signs: *The Six Bells* or *The Five Bells*, or in Almeley's case, quite simply *The Bells*.

The clock is the work of Smiths of Derby and was installed c.1929, and its chimes add to the atmosphere of the village. Earlier parishioners had to rely on the medieval sundial, vestiges of which are now in the west face of a buttress supporting the south wall of the chancel.

Pevsner was impressed by the stained glass of the chancel east window, describing it as being very convincing early sixteenth century, though made in 1865. There is an equally attractive window in the south wall of the sanctuary. The restoration of 1868 saw the passing of the west gallery, box pews, the royal coat of arms, and panels whereon were written, in accordance with the canons of 1604, the ten commandments, the Lord's prayer, and the Apostles' creed. But it was all done with a degree of sensitivity. What was still serviceable of the old box pews and Jacobean panelling was reused, some on the stalls in front of the front pews, some in the vestry, some in the roof of the north aisle, and some as panelling along the walls. The design of the new pews and stalls anticipates the spirit of art nouveau. The appearance of the church's three large Victorian circular brass chandeliers for candles to light the evening services looks much more characteristic of the period. The differing liturgical functions of chancel and nave were once again emphasized by the restoration of a chancel screen. Happily throughout the church the Victorian floor tiles have escaped drowning by carpet, a fate which so many churches have nowadays to endure. Another Victorian feature to have survived is the stone chimney for the stove once in the corner of the north west aisle. A stove was deemed essential to the spiritual comfort of the Victorian worshipper, and some may recollect how the Revd Francis Kilvert went to view the parish church of St Harmons, when he was offered the living, was horrified by there being no stove in the church.

The two manual and pedals organ by Vowles of Bristol, was given in 1905 by Grace Hyett-Warner, surely a relation of the incumbent, the Revd Richard Hyett-Warner, who followed Campbell in 1877, and was something of a clerical historian. He added to his stipend by taking pupils at the Vicarage.

The church was again restored in 1997 when £108,000 was spent on restoration. Of this £29,542 was raised by the parochial church council. Some of the work still looks rather raw, and matching stone seems to have been disdained, but time and weathering will work their magic.

The *Old Vicarage*, was built in the gothick style, with gently pointed sash windows, under dripstones, during the incumbency 1836-63 of William Edwards, MA. It was enlarged to accommodate the growing family of the Revd William Campbell and the Victorian iron gates, hung on particularly elegant iron gate posts, may belong to this period, like the fir tree at the centre the of circular front drive. The modern bijou vicarage, set back, just beyond *Almeley House*, was built during the time of the Revd Cyril George Challenger, MA, 1967-70, and is now an *Old Vicarage* in its own right, the parish of Almeley now being part of the Eardisley group.

In Salter's opinion it is here, at the *Manor House*, or as is more probable, its manorial predecessor, that we should look for the home of Almeley's most famous son, Sir John Oldcastle, the Lollard martyr, and model for Shakespeare's Falstaff. His name has traditionally connected him with one of the castles, but neither of them would still have been in use when Henry V executed him in 1417. The Lollards, with John Wyclif as their prophet and John Oldcastle as their most eminent local disciple, flourished in west Hereford, rejecting the authority of priests and seeking the reform of the Church.

Besides Sir John Oldcastle, another son of Almeley also achieved an entry in the *Dictionary of National Biography*. He is the Labour politician William George Glenvil Hall, 1887-1962. Born at Almeley in 1887, he was the eldest of the five children of William and Elizabeth Hall, devout Quakers. Educated at the Friends' School, Saffron Walden, he then worked in London as a clerk in various branches of Barclay's Bank. However, his 'lifelong devotion to the needs of the poor, the weak, and the unfortunate' led him to enter Parliament. He did so briefly in 1929, but became the member for many years for the Yorkshire seat of Colne Valley in 1939, by which time he had qualified as a barrister. In the Atlee administration of 1945 Hall served as Financial Secretary to the Treasury under Hugh Dalton and Sir Stafford Cripps. A Privy Councillor, he also represented Britain at the Assembly of the United Nations, and for a short while was chairman of the Parliamentary Labour Party.

By the beginning of the seventeenth century the Pembers of Newport, or *Nieuport*, to use the original spelling, were the chief landowners in the parish of Almeley. They remained so until 1712 when the estate was sold to Thomas Foley, a Worcestershire iron-master, ennobled the previous year. He died in 1733. The house was rebuilt in 1774 when its timber-framed predecessor 'of many gables and many eras' was replaced by what Robinson considered to be 'a handsome modern mansion of greater uniformity but lesser interest'.

Robinson was writing in 1872 and the 1774 house, built with three three-storey bays, the central one being surmounted by a pediment, had been recently enlarged. The original house was balanced on each side by the addition of a two-storey pavilion, each linked to the central block by a single storey extension. Matching bay windows were added to the ground floor, either side of the front entrance, and the original Georgian glazing bars of the house were modified to allow the installation of larger panes of new-fangled plate glass.

When the Hon Andrew Foley, 1750-1818, became master of Newport he 'added much to its beauties, by extending the walks and plantations.' His eldest son, Thomas Foley, 1778-1822, MP for Herefordshire 1807-18, was buried at Almeley where his memorial in the church speaks of him as 'a gentleman celebrated for his hospitality and remarkable for his benevolence of mind and affability of manners'. His spinster sister, Grace Foley, lived on at Newport, but by the marriage of her sister Henrietta Maria, the house and its estates passed to the Onslows. In 1863 it was sold to James Watt Gibson Watt, grandson of James Watt, and one suspects it was he who modernized the house according to the latest Victorian taste. Ten years later, in 1873, a certain Mrs Pease, a Quaker, described as 'the principal landowner and lady of the manor' acquired it. This 'certain Mrs Pease' was probably Francis Edwards of Hindwell, Walton, who married Edward Lucas Pease at the Ross-on-Wye Meeting House, in 1862. Edwin was an Iron-master and member of an influential and wealthy Quaker family from Darlington. His relative, Joseph Pease, in 1832 became the first Member of Parliament to affirm rather than take the oath.

By 1881 the Taylors were living at Newport and doing so in some style. William Francis Taylor described himself that year as a landowner and JP. His family home was Moseley Hall in what are now the southern suburbs of Birmingham. This elegant house, built in 1791, became the home of Richard Cadbury, who gave it in 1890 to be a children's home. At Newport, Taylor, still Lord of the Manor of King's Norton, lived with his wife Augusta and their children with the assistance of a butler, footman, hall boy, three stable boys, house keeper, nurse, three housemaids, kitchen maid, scullery maid lodgemaid, and Mademoiselle Floristine Bunot from Paris, who seems to have been a prototype of the *au pair*, as a governess.

Times changed, however, and after the Great War Herefordshire County Council bought Newport for a sanatorium, with plans at the same time to divide the estate into thirty-eight smallholdings for ex-servicemen. After the Second World War Newport was occupied by exiled Latvians. But as their numbers dwindled, the upkeep of such a large house became beyond their resources and it has recently been sold and is being restored as a private house.

When in 1818 the route of the Kington Tramway was planned to make its way to Eardisley by way of Almeley, the legislation prescribed that nothing was to be constructed on the Newport estate and its route took it well to the east of it. The route of the Kington and Eardisley Railway was less constricted and its Almeley station was built on the estate.

———————

Walk 2: Almeley to Eardisley and back.

We set off from the *Bells*: a quintet this time, with mum and dad, infant daughter, riding in a baby back pack carrier on her father's back, grandad, and Gabby. We turned left on leaving the car park, past *Bells Orchard*, down into the village.

Almeley was Herefordshire's best kept village in 1991 and a sign by the well-kept *Memorial Garden* tells you so. The actual war memorial is in the form of a soldier, sculpted in stone, and holding his rifle and looking down in homage on the plinth below carrying the names of his comrades. There are 18 names for the Great War of 1914-18, two of which were those of officers and one of a non-commissioned officer. A good number of them were volunteers, conscription not being introduced until January 1916. On the other hand horses were impressed for gun-teams within a week of the outbreak of war. Few of them returned. There are six names for the Second World War of 1939-1945.

Opposite the memorial garden, make a short diversion by crossing over into the road to Eardisley and Kington. On the right hand side there is an informative commemorative millennium map in bronze, mounted on a plinth. It records that the population of the village is 550: in 1861 it was 637. The village pump is nearby. Just beyond is *Almeley House*, opposite the north side of the church. With its three storeys, in whitewashed brick with large sash windows, and central gable this handsome Georgian residence would not look out of place in a country town. It was built in 1752 as the house of the agent of Newport House, further down the road. Ignored by Pevsner, it is listed as a Grade II building, and claims that after all these years, it has its original front door.

The *Manor House*, a little further on, and on the same side of the road, is timber-framed with brick infilling. It has a two-storeyed gabled porch, added to the medieval original c.1500. It looks appropriately antique with its bulging and irregular walls. There is a splendid stone wall to the garden. *Manor Cottage* on other side of the road, is also timber framed with brick infill. Now turn back towards the memorial garden, with the parish church on your right. Then turn right at the T-junction on to the road to Kinnersley. Pass *Church House*, stuccoed primrose and cheerful, with central sash windows and casements at either end. Further down the road is *Castle Frome Farm* whose antiquity is assured by its cruck trusses and has an interesting name. The Somerset place-name *Frome*, and its Herefordshire counterparts *Bishop's*, *Canon*, and *Castle Frome* all commemorate a river so named. It is British in origin and is identical to the Welsh form of *Ffraw* which appears on Anglesey, as in *Aberffraw*. It means fair, fine, or brisk. The Newport Estate map of 1774 shows a plot of land near Castle Frome Farm, which was called *Mill Orchard* suggesting the proximity of a water mill. Perhaps the stream that worked the mill, and is now no more than a brook, was once known as the Frome.

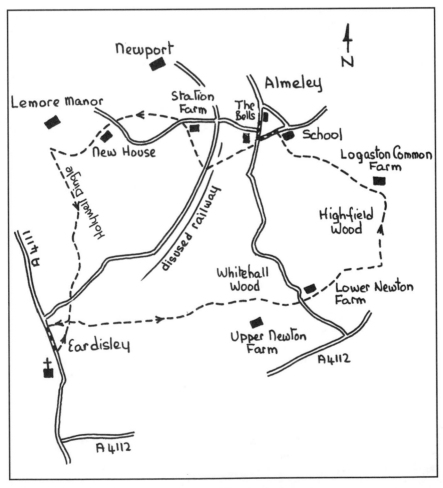

But we are getting off course, and we have to cross the road, just past the church, cross an old fashioned stile, and you are in grounds of Almeley castle. Work your way to the left of the earthen remains of the old motte and bailey, and the long dry fish ponds, and give a moment to the handsome parish church to your right. It is large for a village such as this and reflects the prosperity of the community it served in medieval times. It is still full to over flowing for the observance of those rites of passage like weddings and funerals, which still bring the community together. As we passed there was a very large funeral indeed, obviously of a farmer, for we could hear the robust strains of *We plough the fields and scatter* being sung by the mourners. Literally appropriate, too, for the grain was ripening in the fields beyond on this afternoon in mid-August.

Past the earthworks cross over a stile, which is also a bridge, a rather sophisticated wooden structure, erected, as a notice says, by the Kington Footpath Scheme and the Open Spaces Society. It crosses the diminutive stream of the Frome. Excellent for pedestrians, but mighty difficult for quadrupeds, and sadly one has to admit that these walks are far from being dog friendly. Gabby has to be carried over most of the stiles, and there have been very few with dog gates. Most dogs could get through the traditional stile were it not for the prevalent custom of blocking them with wire netting.

An arrow at the end of the bridge directs one diagonally left through the pasture where we had the curious attention of a herd of rather pretty bullocks, though it was uncomfortably pressing at times, as they breathed heavily down our necks. A stile awaits on the other side of the field. Follow the arrow to the next stile on the other side of the field. A capricious farmer had raised the height of this stile so that it demanded some determined athleticism to get over it. The field had been subdivided with a new fence not on the ordnance survey map. Leaving the stile behind us, we walked right around the margin of the field until we came to the gate leading into the next field. Looking back there was a lovely view of the wooded slopes of Ladylift. Cross the field to the next stile where stinging nettles and thistles abounded. These are plainly not walks for those with a sartorial taste for shorts. Over the stile follow the direction of the yellow arrow through an apple orchard. Another stile, cross it, and the yellow arrow directs us to the left. Then, once over another stile, a short distance to the left along the bed of what was once the Kington and Eardisley Railway, where a stile takes one to the Almeley-Eardisley road.

A tramway linking Kington and Eardisley, with the motive power supplied by horses, opened in 1820.

The idea of replacing it with a railway, with steam locomotives, was first discussed at a public meeting in Kington at *the Oxford Arms* in April 1862. But it did not open until August 1874 and was never a financial success. Its promoters should have paid heed to advice given them by Brunel that their ideas were unwise and impolitic. The Almeley platform and station building still survive, the latter, ivy clad, serves as a farm building, and has given its name to the adjacent *Station Farm*, one of the farms established after the Great War when the Newport estate was broken up.

The line's stations, though stone built with roofs of slate, were very modest affairs and offered their stationmasters no accommodation. According to the census returns, in 1881 twenty-four year old John Buckland was the stationmaster of Almeley. He came from Scotland and he and his wife shared their home with their deaf and dumb brother in law, who made boots and shoes. The railway offered work to several of the sons of Almeley. The level crossing keeper, for example, in 1881, lived alone in *The Hut*. He was 47, but the emphasis was on youth, and besides the young stationmaster, there was also Thomas Powell, a twenty year old plate layer, living with his wife and eleven month son at *Green Cottage*.

But to return to the walk. Across the Almeley road there is a public footpath sign and a stile waiting to be crossed. Follow the yellow arrow and beyond a stout oak tree there is a stile to take you beyond. Past the water trough for the cattle, another arrow directs one ahead across the next field. Cross quite a small field to the far corner diagonally to the right where another stile awaits. Pass a dead oak on the right, through the gate and turn immediately to the left and follow the hedge. To the right you will see *Station Farm* and the derelict railway station is a little beyond it, and out of sight.

Following the arrows you will arrive at a stile which on the day of our walk was almost totally overwhelmed with nettles. Cross it and the Kington-Almeley road, turning right and then after a few yards turn left into the drive which leads to *Newport*. The fortunes of *Newport* are still looked after by its original octagonal single storey stuccoed gothick lodge and porch, guarding the entrance to the drive. Without its modern additions the eighteenth century gate-keeper and his family lived very confined lives.

Just past the Lodge, with its post box, and a few yards up the drive, on the left, is a signpost taking you through a gate. Cross the field diagonally to the right, then across the next field diagonally to your left [which means in fact you continue in a straight line in the same direction] and on diagonally to the right across the next field to its corner. You get a glimpse of Newport amongst the trees, and then through a little gate one is in the top margin of

Coke's Yeld Dingle. More about Dr Coke and his family later, for the present it may be of interest that the Old English *gield*, denotes a payment or tax, which had to be made on the dingle. Follow a farm track through the trees towards the left, and to the right there is a still lake carrying reflections of *Newport*. It was part of the landscaped gardens for which Newport was once famous.

Pass Newport lake, following the grassy farm track, the going is quite rough, until coming to a stile, with an arrow directing one on ahead into a field. In so doing we followed the field round, with the hedge on our right. A stile, notwithstanding an electric fence, eventually meets you, with an iron gate to its left. There is a pond to the left, and after a short distance there is another gate well protected by stinging nettles. Carry on, with hedge still to the right, cross the field, through the gate, across the Kington-Almeley road once again. The signed footpath now goes through the yard of *New House Farm*. We were asked to dip our shoes in the bath of disinfectant before going through a gate into the yard. There is a farm shop and very tempting home made ice cream is for sale. Pass the brick-built farmhouse on the left.

In the second half of the 19th century brick began to displace timber framing in Almeley's house building. Hence *Brick Cottage* and the records tell of brick-burning as the occupation of James Fast of *Meer*, and bricklaying as the work of others. The arrival of the railway also facilitated the availability of mass produced bricks.

At the end of the yard there is large gate with a directing yellow arrow. A courteous notice makes the reasonable request that the public should keep its dog on a lead, to keep to the right of way, and close the gate. We are now in a gently descending farm lane, rather muddy, when we used it. Hedges on both sides are rich in wild flowers, ferns, blackberries and hazel nuts. There is a gate at the end the lane and an arrow pointing the direction ahead diagonally, across a blocked-up cattle grid into a field where, immediately to the left there is a stile. Over it, and travelling slightly diagonally to the right, *Lemore Manor* can been seen amongst the trees to the far right.

Lemore Manor was the home of the Coke family, already encountered in *Coke's Yeld Dingle*. Though previously known as *Low Moor* and *The Moor*, one suspects that the original name was Welsh, something like *Ty Mawr*, the *Big House*, which is fitting enough. Certainly *Low Moor* is inappropriate on the slopes of Bollingham and the antiquity of the site is indicated by the archaeological evidence of a moat slightly to the north of the house.

In 1642 Lemore was the home of Dr George Coke, bishop of Hereford in 1636-46. 'A grave and studious man, well beloved in his diocese', Coke was one of the ten bishops imprisoned in the Tower of London in 1641 on a charge of treason brought against them by the Puritan minded House of Commons. For eighteen months George Coke languished in prison, and it was not long after his return to Hereford that the civil war broke out between Charles I and Parliament in August 1642. The Puritan victory saw the dispossession of George Coke as bishop of Hereford and the suppression of episcopacy and the temporary triumph of presbyterianism. Coke retired to Lemore where he died in December 1646. He was buried in Eardisley parish church.

But history has its ironies. George Coke suffered for his opposition to Puritanism, personified locally by Sir Robert Harley of Brampton Bryan. But two centuries later, one of George Coke's descendants,

the Revd George Coke, MA, 1797-1863, of Lemore, was presented, Anglicanism having been long restored, to the Harley living of Aylton, near Ledbury. The clerical tradition of Lemore was continued by the Revd Francis Coke, MA, who inherited the manor and became vicar of Titley in 1877. His brother, Major General Sir John Coke, 1807-1897, KCB, JP, DL, of the Bengal Army, survived the Indian Mutiny of 1857, and lived at Lemore in his retirement. He is commemorated in Eardisley church. The Coke family retained *Lemore* into the twentieth century, but it is now a nursing home, and is known as *Campbell House Nursing Home*. The present building is early Victorian, in a somewhat gothick idiom, with sash windows under dripstones, and pointed windows in the attic gables.

En route again, on the left, beyond the fence, is *Holywell Dingle*. A finger post on the left offers the choice of three directions. We followed the direction over the stile into *Holywell Dingle*. The name takes us back to the days long before the National Health Service. For centuries the poor relied upon folk medicine and the waters of the dingle were no doubt both thought and found to be efficacious in a multitude of maladies. The dingle is now in the care of the Herefordshire Nature Trust, founded in 1962.

The Trust is the leading local force for wildlife in Herefordshire. This Wildlife Trust is one of a network of 46 registered charities throughout the United Kingdom, working to protect wildlife for the future. Even in Herefordshire the destruction of hedgerows, the pollution of rivers and streams, the ploughing up of meadows, and the neglect of woodland streams threaten the county's wildlife. Irrevocable losses include the disappearance of the *marsh fritillary*, and the departure of the secretive *water rail*, and the *corncrake*.

Over the stile, turn immediately left over another one, so that one is back-tracking on the other side of the fence one had just come by. The path drops down into the dingle which when we walked on our August day was rich in foliage, ferns, wild flowers, and welcome shade. A finger post offers the choice of carrying straight on, or of turning right. We carried on until we arrived at another T-junction. Here we bore right and the stream is also on the right below in the dingle. Ignore a gate on the right, which would have taken you across the stream, but continue on. A post with a yellow arrow will direct you to the left and to ascend quite a steep slope. Arriving eventually at a stile, cross it and follow the direction of the arrow straight on, the path rising gently, and bearing to the left. At the summit another post tells you to carry on, down a steep path, the stream still on the right. Eventually we arrived at a single sided footbridge across the stream. *Please close the gate* we are bidden as we leave the Dingle at the end of the footbridge.

The gently rising footpath now takes us through a field, wooded on either side. An arrow advises us to follow the fencing on the left. Beyond the fence Holywell Dingle, which we have left, continues for some distance. Lovely views of the Wye Valley and Bredwardine Hill extended before us, with the Black Mountains to the right. Arriving at a gate on the other side of the field, pass into the next field, the arrow directing us across it. On the map it appears as a large isosceles triangle, and we cross it with the apex to our left and then follow on the fence to its base. This brings us to the Almeley Road, with the encroaching environs of Eardisley to the right. Cross the road to another stile giving access to a straight avenue on a slight embankment, which carried the Tramway, now nearing the end of its eight miles and one furlong run from Kington. Today it is the playground of rabbits. Passing a footbridge on the left, cross a stile just beyond it to the right, and leaving the avenue, cross in the direction of the arrow towards the village. The path will take you along the side of a stream, into the village street. Here we turned right, over the little bridge, and on towards Kington, admiring the medley of black and white houses, village hall, and shops until we were confronted with the choice of taking refreshment. One kind was on offer at *The Tram Inn,* on the other side of the street, and another at *The New Strand* licensed bar, coffee house, and second hand bookshop, which was opposite. On this occasion we opted for tea and books in the garden.

Duly refreshed we left the *New Strand*, turning left into the main street of the village. Eardisley, though being murdered by heavy lorries, is well worth a visit in its own right. As David Verey put it:

> The village compactly lines a single street with a fair proportion of black and white houses. It is the centre of a large parish in which medieval farm houses abound, hidden away in the orchards.

We crossed over the stream and then went on past the footpath by which we arrived in the village. Passing black and white cottages with such names as *Jasmine Cottage*, *The Old Police Station*, *Birds Wood*, *Pine Tree Cottage*, *Pilgrim Cottage*, and *Drey Cottage*, all with luxuriant gardens. Then, to provide variety, on the other side of the street was *Lower House*. Then past *Burgoyne's Garage*, rather less than elegant and with a rake of Japanese vehicles for sale in the forecourt, for this is the 21st century and not the 15th. Then comes a new housing development, in red brick and pebble-dash, and cottagey. In the middle of this development, just before *Millstream Gardens*, a reminder that the medieval village was self-contained and used the lord's mill to grind its corn for its daily bread, follow the footpath sign to the left.

Beyond, on the other side of the road, is the parish church, worthy of a visit, and to the right of the lychgate, there is on the wall a helpful information board about the village. Being far briefer, it might prove particularly interesting to those who have neither time nor inclination to read the historical account of Eardisley in this book.

But to return to the footpath sign just before *Millstream Gardens*, and the walk to Almeley. This footpath takes you through the new houses, and one is suddenly walking through Eardisley's answer to *Brookside*. Follow the tarmac path through this suburban orderliness until you arrive at a stile. Over it, then turn left, following the arrows, into a field with a stile and an iron gate: wooden five bar gates are a rarity nowadays indeed. Cross the field, diagonally to the right, to arrive at the far corner. We are now in familiar territory through which we passed earlier on our way into the village. Cross the style, with its welcome DIY dog entry, for which Gabby was very grateful. It does little for the dignity of a large dog to have to be carried over a succession of stiles, and there were times when she protested.

We are now in the avenue of trees, once the path of the tramroad. But not for long, and almost immediately turn right over a dog-friendly footbridge and cross the open field with the hedge to your right. At the far right hand corner of this meadow a stile, again dog friendly in the form of another footbridge, awaits us. Then, following the direction of the yellow arrow, cross the next field. This takes you under electricity cables carried on poles, and one is reminded how the advent of electricity has transformed rural life. The authors lived ten years in a Radnorshire vicarage, wherein electricity had but recently been installed, and the vicar's ability to mend a fuse was thought to be a rare, almost spiritual, accomplishment. But that was a world in which the Tilley lamp still prevailed.

A yellow arrow now takes us through a gate and over the empty track bed of the Kington and Eardisley Railway which at this stage was nearing the end of its journey.

We did this walk in August and it was on 4th August 1874 that the first train ran between Kington and Eardisley. It left Kington at 12 20 pm and its arrival at Eardisley was celebrated by an *al fresco* lunch in a field near the station. The return trip conveyed Mr Justice Quain *en route* for Presteign Assizes. Sir John Richard Quain, QC, 1816-1876, was an Irishman with a spirit of adventure and a confidence in the reliability of the railway which few would share today if they hoped to open the assizes on time. He became a judge in the Queen's Bench division in 1871.

By 1890 the Kington and Eardisley Railway Company owed the Great Western Railway, which had worked the line from its opening for half the profits, £5,190. Understandably the GWR was reluctant to continue the arrangement. In 1897 the GWR bought the Kington Company, then in liquidation, for £45,000. In 1916 the GWR, as part of the war effort, closed the line and took up the track. Folk tradition has it that it was to be relaid in war-stricken France, but the ship carrying it there was sunk by an enemy submarine.

In 1920 the Herefordshire County Council made representations to the GWR for relaying the track. The company was resistant, but promised the line would be reinstated when the necessary materials were available. This was done in 1922 and the occasion this time was marked, not by a picnic in the fields at Eardisley, but by an informal luncheon at Kington's *Burton Hotel*.

The reopened railway offered a passenger service of three trains in each direction a day, one of which was a mixed goods *and* passenger train. Travel by this train was a triumph of hope over experience, such was the degree of shunting required at Almeley and Lyonshall stations to attach and detach cattle and coal trucks, whilst the passengers waited patiently in their none too comfortable four wheeled carriages. These lacked corridors or any of the conveniences of the modern eight-wheeled railway carriage. The outbreak of the Second World War gave the GWR the opportunity it had been waiting for, and in the name of economy and helping the war effort, the line was finally closed in July 1940. The track was again taken up, and the buildings and land sold.

———————————

Over the dismantled railway, follow the arrow and walk ahead, towards two mature oak trees, across this field which on the map appears as a right-angled triangle. Access to the next field is by another stile, with something of a ditch in front of it. Once over, keep to the right, along which, beyond a rudimentary stream, there is a line of mature trees, forming, as it were, an emasculated linear copse, affording welcome shade. Near the corner of the field a stile can be found to the left, and soon afterwards, a dog-friendly foot-bridge takes you through the hedge and over a stream. The yellow arrow at the end of the bridge directs us straight on to the stile in the hedge ahead. It was well protected by brambles and nettles, and the arrow directed our path across the new field, with the hedge on our right. The sun shone gloriously for us, but infant Emma riding in her back pack, rather in the manner of an Indian *howdah*, her father being the elephant, takes a wilful delight in discarding her sun-hat at moments she deems she will be least observed. This prolongs the walk with hunt-the-hat episodes, which hitherto, have all been successful.

Another stile ahead of us at the other side of the field, is crossed and once again the arrow directs us to continue ahead. On the map this public foot-path looks remarkably straight in its course all the way from Eardisley, though it is often tempting to make deviations, *around* a field rather than going *across* it, as the map suggests, to avoid damaging growing crops. Do not, for legal reasons, do this, and always keep to the footpath.

With a hedge and trees on our right we follow on across the field. A farmer is working away in a combine harvester. With hazard lights flashing and alone in the air-conditioned cab of this magnificent machine, one realises again how agriculture has changed from the labour intensive industry it once was. A hundred and fifty years ago, the farms, admittedly quite large, of four hundred acres or more, were worked by the master and his sons, together with perhaps eight labourers and a boy or two. There were also specialist waggoners, cowmen, and shepherds. The records show that women labour-ers were not uncommon either, and this was long before the Women's Land Army was brought in during the Second World War. The mechanical predecessor of the tractor was the traction engine of the 1870s, but the horse had its place until after the second war.

In the far right hand corner a conventional stile waits for us. We are now in an apple orchard, remembering that the logo for Herefordshire is a cider apple, and that May is the time here for acres and acres of apple-blossom. Once through the orchard a stile takes us into a paddock, quite small.

Whitehall Wood is to the left and to the right the buildings can be seen of *Upper Newton Farm*. This is an early 17th century farm house of substance, to which further additions were made in the 18th century. Its moulded beams reflect the status of those who lived there. That status continued, too; in 1883 the master described himself as a 'gentleman farmer'.

Over the stile turn left and bear diagonally to the right, through another orchard, from whence an iron gate leads into another field. Bear left now, past a great oak tree, and a yellow arrow shows the way through a little gate. This takes us through a small paddock, and leaving it, cross the Kinnersley-Almeley road, and enter the yard of *Lower Newton Farm*, passing the stone-built farm house, with old brick extensions, on your right. There are farm buildings of some antiquity to your left. Ahead a stile gives access to a grassy lane. Bulmers orchards lie ahead and it is the age of scientific cider making, so we are asked 'In the interests of hygiene please keep your dogs on a lead. Do not let them foul the orchards'.

There are extensive orchards on either side of the lane. Some way down this lane a finger post offers the choice of carrying on ahead, or of turning off to the right. Carry on here, and on arriving at a modern agricultural building, turn right and continue until you arrive at a hedge where in an opening there is a stile, and once over it, the yellow arrow points the way to the left.

This takes you past, on the right hand side, a nursery of apple trees, bearing such labels as *Newton Wonder*, *Red Norman*, *Lord Suffield*, and *Yellow Ingestrie*. With the fence on your left, follow its course round. Arriving at a footbridge on the left, cross it. Reassuringly, it carried a notice: *This Public Right of Way is now open*. Memories of the extent and length of the Foot and Mouth epidemic of 2001 will long be remembered.

Follow the tree-lined margin of the field on the left. Now there comes another bridge, with a stile beyond. This takes us very briefly into *Highfield Wood*. But one soon comes to another stile and bridge, leading into another orchard, with *Highfield Wood* now to the right, with its badger gates set in the fence. Ignore a gate into the wood on your right, carry straight on between the apple trees and when confronted by a fence turn left. Follow the direction of the arrows and you will arrive at a stile and bridge which leads through a paddock. Past *Little Logaston*, turn left into a lane, rather than continuing along it to *Logaston Common Farm*.

Pass a timber framed house with brick in-filling on the right with its attendant farm buildings, and follow the track, not getting diverted by branch tracks leading off to nearby houses. Bear to your right past another house surrounded by a high hedge, the path steadily descending. A wooden footbridge takes us over a stream. A Persian cat, sitting on the handrail, guarded the bridge when we arrived, but after some hesitation, it diplomatically avoided a confrontation with Gabby, and withdrew. A short distance ahead one arrives at a stile with a dog gate. Follow the direction of the yellow arrow. Over the stile, bear right and you will arrive at an arrow-signed iron gate. Go through it, the arrow pointing to the left, following the hedge until arriving at a stile and bridge over a brook, which no doubt swells considerably in winter. In the distance to the left can be seen the Black Mountains. Cross the field to the new wire fence ahead with a stile and yellow arrow. Make for the double stile ahead in the well kept hedge, taking you over a ditch, once over, follow the arrow pointing ahead. A couple of stiles in the far right hand corner of this field take us into the next one where a stile and footbridge in the left hand corner takes us into the last field of the walk.

Ahead, peeping above the final hedge, is Almeley Primary School, built in 1850 for £670, which the local School Board had to borrow from the government, and repay. In those days there were 80 children on the roll. The awe-inspiring views of the Black Mountains enjoyed by the pupils must surely have enriched greatly the value of their education.

The last stile of the walk, with a dog board, [*Euge!* We all shout, for Gabby is well versed in Latin], gives access to the Almeley-Sarnesfield road. Turn left towards Almeley. Arriving at a T-junction, with Almeley parish church ahead, turn right, up the hill, past *Church House* and the *War Memorial*, both now familiar sights, until you arrive at the *Bells*.

EARDISLEY

The Victorians wrote of Eardisley as a village

> Situated in a valley below Kingswood and Bollingham, in the midst of scenery of a beautiful character, enriched by plantations, luxuriant orchards, and gentlemen's seats.

Modern commentators are rather more prosaic, noting that the village has a proper street. This is not all that frequent in Herefordshire, though Pembridge comes immediately to mind. Once again the origins of the parish are pre-Norman and Ekwall considered the place-name commemorated Ægheard's *leah*, or clearing in the woods. Domesday records that Robert de Baskerville held the lordship from Roger de Lacy and mentions too, in a significant passing reference to Norman society, that there were at Eardisley two slaves and one Welshman. As was the case at Huntington, so at Eardisley the lordship was divided into a lowland Englishry and an upland Welshry.

Domesday mentions there being a *domus defensabilis*, a fortified house, at Eardisley. This was the ancestor of the castle and what little of it still survives can be seen to the west of the church. These remains consist of a roughly oval moated enclosure, with a motte, some 33½ yards in diameter at its base, and rising 14ft above the present level of the bailey. The motte stands in the south west corner of the bailey, and the surrounding moat encloses an area of about 1½ acres. There was an outer enclosure to the west of these remains. A small borough grew up around the protection of the castle and in 1233 a licence was granted for a fair and market. A pleasure and hiring fair on May 15th survived well into the second half of the 19th century.

The de Bohuns as Earls of Hereford followed the de Lacys as overlords of Eardisley until 1372, but the castle was occupied by tenants and in 1263 Roger de Clifford was in possession. It was here that Peter D'Aigueblanche, bishop of Hereford 1240-68, was imprisoned in 1264. Archdeacon of Salop before becoming bishop of Hereford, D'Aigueblanche came from Savoy and was rewarded with the bishopric by Henry III for his useful financial services to the state. He established his nephew John D'Aigueblanche as dean of

Hereford and welcomed both relatives and fellow countrymen to the diocese with preferment. Up to the Reformation bishoprics, deaneries, and archdeaconries were often occupied by clerics from the Continent. The universal ecclesiastical use of Latin meant that language was no problem.

In 1262 Llywelyn ap Gruffydd, grandson of Llywelyn the Great, ravaged the Herefordshire lowlands as far as Weobley and Eardisley, and Peter D'Aigueblanche, fearing, as a royal partizan, for his safety, betook himself to Gloucester. Henry III had himself just returned from France and was in feeble health, but he was not impressed by the absence of the bishop and his clergy from their cathedral when he came to Hereford to organise his forces for a Welsh campaign. Threatened with Henry's anger and the loss of their stipends, Peter D'Aigueblanche and his clergy returned to Hereford, only to be attacked and captured by a coalition of barons under Roger Clifford who removed him and his Savoyard canons to Eardisley castle. D'Aigueblanche was imprisoned here for three months, but was eventually paid 300 marks in compensation. Rather than return to his palace at Hereford, the bishop went to his manor at Stretton Sugwas where he died on 27th November 1268, having made his will the day before.

In 1272 William Baskerville was licensed to have services in the chapel of Eardisley castle which was by now the principal residence of the Baskervilles. In June 1309 Miles Pychard of Staunton-on-Wye complained that Walter de Baskerville assaulted him near Letton, and that Peter le Taillur, constable of of Eardisley castle, and others

> issuing from that castle, approaching his manor of Staunton, broke the doors and locks of his houses, and killed Richard de Shorham, whom they found there.

The castle enjoyed some revival of status in the early 15th century when Henry IV ordered Nicholas Montgomery to fortify the castle against the ravages of ubiquitous Owain Glyndwr in 1403. Owain Glyndwr, c.1354-c.1416, Prince of Wales and national hero, his 1402 victory over Edward Mortimer at the battle of Pilleth still fresh, was at the height of his powers. There were doubtless many in the Lordship of Eardisley, proud of their Welsh ancestry, who wished Glyndwr well.

Most of the castle was demolished during the Civil War, and the fortunes of the Baskervilles were in such decline that the last of the Eardisley branch of the family had to be content to live in poverty in the gate house. In 1670 the estate passed to William Barnesley. The ruined castle was abandoned and by the early 18th century the house and buildings of *Castle Farm* had been established nearby, but it is neither timber framed nor of stone salvaged from the castle, but of brick, plain and nicely proportioned. Its shell-shaped hood over the front door and some surviving windows with their original mullions and transoms add to its charm. It also has some handsome farm buildings, and a six-bay black and white barn has been converted into much sought after houses.

Early in the 18th century the Barnesleys built themselves a new house, *Eardisley Park*, set apart from the village, and a mile to the west of the church. Originally of five bays and two storeys, a third was added in the late 18th century. Its square dovecote, cider-house, and other farm buildings reflect the self-sufficient character of the 18th century country house. Pigeons were valued for their meat, eggs, feathers, down, and dung. They have the advantages of foraging for their own food, a strong homing instinct, mating for life, and producing numerous offspring. The house of course would have ample wine cellars, and besides making sufficient cider for all its needs, the 18th and 19th century country house was not above making its own gooseberry and elderberry wines. Severely damaged by a recent fire, the house is now being restored without its third floor, to the general advantage of its appearance.

William Barnesley, Master of the Clothworkers Company in 1715, invested much of his wealth derived from a long and prosperous career in the City of London. Eardisley was but one of the several estates he acquired in the counties of Hereford, Brecon, and Radnor, most of which were formerly in Baskerville hands. When William's only son, William junior, died unmarried in 1704 Barnesley senior sold his Eardisley estate to his cousin, another William Barnesley, a Bencher of the Inner Temple. He made Eardisley Park his country seat and was Sheriff of Herefordshire in 1704. His son, yet another William, in 1723, when he was 19, fell in love with Elizabeth Price of Clyro, and though she was yet 13, they contrived to get married. This was done with the connivance of Mrs Price in London, before the provisions of Lord Hardwicke's Marriage Act of 1753 whereby marriage by affirmation before witnesses was no longer legally recognized.

The errant William's father on discovering what had happened banished him to Ireland, even though Elizabeth Price had a substantial dowry of £500 besides property. Old Mr Barnesley died suddenly at a great age in 1737, and by then his son was showing signs of insanity. At this juncture a Hereford lawyer, Mansel Powell of Wellington, produced a will in which William Barnesley left the bulk of the estate to him. In 1744 Mrs Barnesley had her husband certified insane. She also established that the will produced by

Powell was a forgery and that her husband was the legal heir to all his father's real estate in the counties of Hereford, Radnor, Brecon, Middlesex, and Hertford. These were valued at £1,700 per annum, and the father's personal estate was valued at £60,000. Thus a very wealthy Mrs Barnesley entered into residence at Eardisley Park, whilst her husband languished in a private asylum.

There was some embarrassment in 1753 when William Barnesley's insanity, [which he could not help, and not, as recorded on the list of incumbents in the church, his indulgence in simony, which he could have helped] made him unable to nominate an incumbent to the vacant living. Instead the Crown presented the Revd Richard Coke, BA, thereby keeping alive the local Coke connection.

William Barnesley died in 1760 and was buried in Eardisley church, Powell was sent to Hereford gaol for life, and Elizabeth Barnesley in her troubles turned to Methodism for comfort, enjoying the friendship and support of Howell Harris of Trefecca. Later she married Marmaduke Gwynne of Garth and Llanelwedd, a committed Methodist, and when she died in 1773 she left £2,000 to Selina, Countess of Huntington, to support her Methodist seminary at Trefecca.

The Barnesleys memorial in the vestry of Eardisley church makes bitter reading:

> From the death of his Father they were involved in tedious Law
> suits for Thirty Five Years to the great prejudice of their health
> and Estates: at length they overcame and died conquerors.

But not quite, and five years more litigation ensued after Elizabeth Barnesley's death in 1773. It was eventually established that the rightful heirs to the Barnesley estate were the descendants of three daughters of the William Barnesley who had bought Eardisley Park in the first place. With some dispatch Eardisley Park was sold to a Dr JL Petit of London who, in turn, sold it to James Perry, a Wolverhampton merchant whose daughter Mary married Thomas Bainbrigge Herrick, also of Wolverhampton. Their only son, William Perry-Herrick was born in 1794, and educated at Rugby and Oxford, was called to the bar at Gray's Inn in 1821. He inherited Eardisley Park from his father and in 1832 by succeeding his uncle acquired Beaumanor Park, near Loughborough, in Leicestershire. Forsaking Eardisley, he made his home at Beaumanor and was High Sheriff for Leicestershire in 1835 and a JP and DL for the county as well. His membership of the Carlton Club reflects his political sympathies. Eardisley Park became the home of a succession of tenant farmers.

William Perry-Herrick was very generous to Eardisley. In 1857 he gave the land and met the cost of building a new school to replace the 'small stone building' which had served as the parish's Sunday and day school for some 30 boys and girls. The education it offered was modest, the master doubling as clerk and sexton to parish church, with bell ringing and grave-digging as part of his responsibilities. All the same, he was continuing a tradition first recorded at Eardisley in 1548 when William Dayson *kept scole.* Established as a National School, with a professionally trained master, the new 1857 school, built in brick opposite the church, was much larger than its immediate predecessor, and was further enlarged in 1870.

In 1866 it cost £136.7s.1d. to run the school, which the Eardisley historian David Gorvett calculates to have been £7,125 at today's value. Roughly speaking this was met by the combination in equal proportions of a government grant, public subscriptions, and 'School Pence' paid by the pupils' parents. Herrick also paid the entire cost of the very expensive 1862 restoration of the parish church besides underwriting several parish charities and contributing to the Alms Houses. Finally, it was through him that the rectorial tithes were returned to the church, the incumbents becoming once again rectors rather than vicars.

As the patron of the living, the rectory was in Herrick's gift, and here again one can probably see his influence. In 1866 he presented the long serving Charles Samuel Palmer, MA to the living. An Oxford graduate, it may not have been coincidental that he came from Leicestershire. He was at Eardisley for 40 years, and his photograph, with that of his wife, hangs in the church. He was assisted in the care of his 900 parishioners by a succession of curates, understandably mainly Oxford men. But what is more significant is that they were of the new generation of professionally trained clergymen who had further post-graduate study at one or other of the new theological colleges. The calling of a clergyman of the established Church had hitherto been the prerogative of gentlemen, preferably of private means. But times were changing, and Palmer, perhaps with Herrick's encouragement, chose academically well-qualified men who had also undergone training for the practical demands of being a clergyman. After Oxford, one had gone to Wells Theological College and another to the Leeds Clergy School. Under Palmer Eardisley acquired branches of the Mother's Union and the Girl's Friendly Society, and a Church institute. Both Charles and Ellen Palmer are commemorated by stained glass in the church.

In her long widowhood, Mrs Sophia Perry-Herrick, continued the tradition of interest and support established by her late husband, and when she died in 1915 she was succeeded by William Montagu Curzon-Herrick of Beaumanor Park and Bardon Hall, Leicestershire, who assumed the additional surname of Herrick by royal license in 1916. The wife of the new lord of the manor and patron of the living, whom Curzon-Herrick married in 1916, had the distinction of being none other than Lady Maud Kathleen Cairnes Plantagenet Hastings, eldest daughter of the 14th Earl of Huntington. So things go in circles, for it will be recollected that in 1773 Elizabeth Barnesley bequeathed £2000 to Selina, Countess of Huntington, wife of the 9th Earl. The village hall bears the name of William Curzon-Herrick.

Mr Palmer's parishioners saw their parish church as 'a noble structure of a very ancient date, with stone tower, commanding a splendid view of the country around'. It is dedicated to St Mary Magdalene who has 187 ancient English dedications, besides a college bearing her name at both Oxford and Cambridge. Her dedication stands 13th in order of popularity.

Set in a well kept churchyard, with access by a Victorian lych gate, erected in 1862 in memory of the Revd Henry Clelan, who was Vicar from 1859 until his death in 1861, Eardisley parish church is an interesting and complex building. It reflects the evolution and continuity of Christian worship in a rural community from the twelfth century to the present day. It is welcoming, too, to the modern visitor. When we came, the door, beyond the wrought iron gates of the porch, installed apparently in 1848, when William Bufton of *Lady Arbour Farm* and John Edwards of *Upper House Farm* were churchwardens, was open in expectation, as it were, of our coming. By coincidence, even the organ was being played and someone was busily polishing the pews, and both organist and cleaning lady bade us welcome. There is an informed and well-produced church guide on sale.

The oldest part of the church is the present nave, which is thought by Salter to have been built c.1150-60, and to have constituted the whole of the Norman church. The great object of interest to have survived from this earliest stage of the building's history is the font. Now by the south door, until 1863 it was in the middle of the west end of the nave. Pevsner saw it as being, with the font of Castle Frome, the most exciting piece of the Herefordshire school of sculpture, on account both of its composition and for its excellent state of preservation. Its elaborate decoration depicts 'warriors in combat, a saint, a large benevolent lion, and Christ rescuing a person from pressing danger'. The fighting warriors are tall and thin, with pointed faces, beards and moustaches, and have been identified as a Ralph de Baskerville and his father-in-law, Lord Drogo of Clifford, whom he is said to have murdered early in the 12th century, during the reign of King John. If so, the font may have been commissioned by Ralph as part of the act of penance whereby he gave Eardisley church and its tithes to Llanthony abbey, founded in 1109. Unfortunately, the early pedigree of the Baskerville family is still a mixture of mythology and fact, but it seems that Ralph was himself murdered in his house 'craftily and by night'.

Towards the end of the 12th century the narrow south aisle was added and to which access was gained by cutting three round-headed arches into the south wall of the original nave, and one more from what was then the chancel. This allowed entry to a chapel at the east end of the new aisle. The north aisle, with a chapel or chapels at the east end; an enlarged chancel; and the south porch followed in the 13th and 14th centuries.

The chancel and chapels, for the sake of reverence and mystery, would all have been enclosed with screens. The great space of the nave, unpewed, was the parish meeting place, as well as its centre of worship. There was colour in wall paintings, gilded and painted screens, and in the vestments of the clergy and frontals of the altars. Over it all hung the crucified Christ, with Mary and John on either side, set up on a broad loft above the chancel screen, access to which was given by a stone staircase inserted into the south side of the chancel arch.

As is well known, the Reformation saw the dissolution of the monasteries and Llanthony was suppressed in 1539, its community of monks having declined to five. This gave the Baskervilles the opportunity to regain the tithes and right to be the patrons of the living of Eardisley. It became the responsibility of the Baskervilles to maintain the north aisle of the church, but in 1675 it was cited as 'ruinous' because the family was not performing its responsibilities. Elsewhere in the church itself, the rood was removed and the chapels and their altars dismantled. The actual chancel screen survived, and would have taken on a new function when the chancel itself became a communion aisle, into which those intending to make their communion moved at the Prayer Book invitation 'to draw near with faith and take this holy Sacrament' to their comfort.

A communion table replaced the high altar, 'fruitful and profitable sentences of holy scripture', as well as the Lord's Prayer, the ten commandments, and the Apostles' Creed adorned the walls instead of wall paintings. The royal coat of arms was displayed over the chancel screen, provoking the Roman

Catholic jibe that 'the dog and the dragon' had supplanted Christ upon the cross. The royal arms had to be renewed at parish expense whenever they changed, and those in use at Eardisley from 1816-1837 have, rather sadly, been banished to the north west corner of the nave where they are now displayed over the entrance to the tower and belfry. They are distinctive in having the arms of Hanover, Brunswick, Luneberg, and Westphalia at the centre of the shield. These were abandoned with the accession of Queen Victoria in 1837.

The tower was rebuilt in 1708 on its original base. It was destroyed by fire, and if it had wooden upper storeys, as at Letton and elsewhere on the Marches, it would have been particularly susceptible to lightning. Five new bells were commissioned in 1708 from Abraham Rudhall the elder of Gloucester for the new tower, to which a sixth was added as a treble in 1887. The frame and headstocks are modern and the bells are said by experienced bell ringers to go well.

In 1862 the church was, they say, thoroughly restored, under the direction of Ewan Christian, 1814-95, whose work was held to be 'distinguished more for its quietness and repose than for architectural effect'. He had been architect to the Ecclesiastical Commissioners since 1850 and was to become president of the Royal Institute of British Architects. He was a friend of Samuel Teulon, the architect of Letton Court, and in earlier days they had gone together on Continental sketching tours. His appointment was no doubt the choice of Perry-Herrick who met the cost of the restoration, £2,450.

Christian, in contrast to Bodley whose influence can be seen at Kinnersley, and Nicholson the diocesan architect, was an evangelical, and this had some influence of the internal form of his restoration. Gorvett relates how most of the building had to be dismantled and rebuilt, and that the roof was totally renewed on account of its failing timbers. All credit here to Christian for roofing both nave and chancel with stone tiles, when slate would have been cheaper but far less sightly. Many of the windows were enlarged. Inside all signs of the 18th century were removed, including the box pews, and the three-decker pulpit. Ceilings were taken down and nothing done to preserve the vestiges of medieval wall paintings when they were uncovered. The font was moved to its present position from the middle of the west end of the nave. The chancel screen and loft, which had survived both Reformation and Commonwealth were removed. The loft, which in its post-Reformation role accommodated the village band and singers, was now redundant. Its place was taken by a new organ by JW Walker, the organ builder favoured by Queen Victoria herself. The instrument has a magnificent screen, which belies its actual modest, one manual, dimensions. It was the gift, made 'In grateful remembrance of the protection of Almighty God in many dangers, especially at Delhi, 1858' by Major General John Coke, of Lemore.

The restored church was reopened for worship on July 3rd 1863, just in time for the inspection of those Cambrian experts who had spent an August day visiting local churches. Unfortunately it was by the time they arrived at Eardisley, towards evening and the day was far spent:

> The excursionists proceeded to Eardisley Church, on their way home. It being dark at the time of arrival, candles were procured from the rectory, by the help of which the singular Norman font... was examined. It is an exceedingly fine example of such Norman work of the twelfth century.

They were probably tired, wanting their supper, and Kington was still a long way by horse-drawn wagonette. Consequently their overall response to Christian's restoration was unenthusiastic:

> The church has been lately restored, at a considerable expense, and seemed to have been well done, as far as could be ascertained by the aid of candles.

Most of the stained glass is late Victorian or Edwardian, in a medieval idiom, and none the worse for that. The modern piece in the south wall of the chancel may, however, excite comment.

There is in the churchyard a restored medieval preaching cross and the war memorial, which instead of naming names and ranks, commemorates with appropriate simplicity, 'the sons of Eardisley.' There are several seats in memory of local citizens for those who want to sit and reflect in this haven away from the traffic of the busy village street. The passing of time is recorded by the tower clock, installed in 1863, it is the work of Reuben Bosworth, of Nottingham. It was needed as much for catching the trains, which had begun to run that year from Hereford to Brecon, as for punctuality in coming to church.

The tithe barns to the north of the church were converted to residential use in 1965. These barns were built to store the large quantities of produce which were paid to the incumbent for his support. He in return was responsible for the maintenance of the church services and for the repair of the chancel. Nonconformist farmers objected to paying for the maintenance of the established church and the clergy themselves found the collection of tithes in kind tedious and a source of friction between them and their parishioners. In 1836 the payment of tithes in kind was converted into a system of monetary payments. The payments of tithes finally disappeared in 1996.

Tramways were a cheaper way of moving goods than canals and the Hay Tramway, which ran from the Brecknock & Abergavenny canal at Brecon reached Hay in 1816 and Eardisley two years later.

Its commercial success moved the principal tradesmen and leading townsmen of Kington to promote its extension from Eardisley on to Kington and the important lime works at Burlingjobb, three and a half miles west of the town.

The act, which had thirty-six promoters, incorporating the Kington company, received the Royal Assent in May 1818. The authorised capital, £18,000, was divided into £100 shares and held by 34 local residents. This amount exactly covered the cost of the line.

The tramway followed a somewhat circuitous route from Kington to Eardisley by way of Lyonshall and Almeley, and was eight miles long instead of the five and a half miles required by a more direct route. Ascending Bollingham, however, 811 feet above sea level, would have involved an average gradient of 1 in 28. The more circuitous route, however, rose no higher than 550 feet above sea level and its maximum gradient was only 1 in 59, an important consideration since the motive power was supplied by horses.

The engineer was John Hodgkinson, who was also the engineer of the Hay Tramway, and the contractors were Hazeldine and Sayce. William Hazeldine was one of Thomas Telford's associates, and Morris Sayce was a Kington surveyor. James Watt, who had an estate at Gladestry, was one of the company's original proprietors, attending their meetings and offering his advice. The tramway, built to the same gauge as its Hay counterpart, 3ft 6ins, to allow trams to be taken through to Brecon, was opened as far as Kington in May 1820. It seems not to have been opened at Burlingjobb until 1833.

Rather in the manner of *Railtrack*, the company provided its clients with track, and the clients paid tolls, conveying their merchandise in their own trams drawn by their own teams of horses. A strict protocol was laid down. The loaded trams were not to weigh more than 2 tons, unless the load was in one piece and trains of trams were not to travel at more than walking pace. When loaded and empty trains met, the empty one had to give way; and when both were loaded the one first reaching the passing post between the passing loops had priority. There was no travelling at night or on Sundays, Christmas Day, Good Friday, or other days of public feast or thanksgiving. No driver was to impede the passage of the tramway for more than fifteen minutes; if he could not repair a defective tram in that time, he was to remove it from the track. The size of the trains was limited to three trams, hauled by two horses.

On Monday, 8th March, 1841, according to Richard Parry, the Kington historian, 'a new machine made its appearance on the Tram-road':

> Two men started from the town of Kington in an ingenious vehicle which they contrived to propel by means of cog-wheels set in motion by a winch, the handles of which were turned by the men who were seated in the machine. They proceeded at the rate of six miles an hour, they reached Brecon the same day, and returned to Hay about five o'Clock on Tuesday with a Ton of Coals; but leaving the machine near the Gas-house whilst they refreshed themselves, some boys began to meddle with the novel affair, and contrived to break one of the wheels, to the great disappointment of the men, who, instead of coming to Kington, which was their intention that night, only reached Eardisley, by pushing the machine before them. A scientific gentleman has stated his conviction, that a machine might be made to suit the purpose of carrying passengers and goods of every description.

No more was heard of the vehicle, which seems to have been some kind of prototype of a ganger's hand trolley or velocipede.

The Kington tramway seems to have been better managed than its Hay counterpart and the dividend it paid varied between 1 and 3%. One of its merits is that coal was made more readily and more cheaply available. According to one of the surviving tramway accounts for the six months ending 29th September 1839, 9,270 tons of coal and coke were carried from which was derived an income of £300 4s 8d. In the other direction, 1,124 tons of lime and limestone were carried for £11 14s 8d, from which it appears the Old Radnor lime works were able to negotiate a very competitive rate for transporting their product in what would have otherwise been empty out-going trams.

In Kington it came to be seriously believed that the Kington tramway 'was the second greatest engineering feat in the world'. But when the Kington and Eardisley Railway acquired it in 1862, it was almost disused, having been unable to compete with the Leominster and Kington Railway which opened in 1857.

The *Tram Inn* was originally a 17th century timber framed building of two storeys, later extended. In 1881 it was under the supervision of Ellen Watkins, a 60-year-old Scottish widow, and she had a strange miscellany of lodgers. Besides two railway workers there were the Savekers and their six children. John Saveker was a saddler and his wife Elizabeth was the local Methodist preacher. Methodism has a strong tradition of total abstinence. Eardisley's Primitive Methodists erected their chapel in 1867 and it was just round the corner from the *Tram* on the Woods Eaves road. The Calvinistic Methodists were in the field earlier, and their chapel, *Great Oak*, was built in 1848 and was originally known as *Tabernacle*. Whilst Mrs Saveker proclaimed the gospel in the cause of the Primitive Methodists, Henry Davies did so on behalf of the Calvinistic Methodists. He came from Breconshire, and he and his wife also had six children, as well as the assistance of resident servant.

The *Tram* commemorates the importance of the tramway to Eardisley in the first half of the 19th century. The horses were stabled here overnight, and no doubt the drivers stayed here as well . The track, as was seen on the walk, ran behind the eastern side of the village.

In the 19th century Eardisley's principal industry, besides farming, and the railways, was making spade trees, one workshop employing 9 men and 4 boys for the task. Other recorded occupations included:

Baker	Maltster
Blacksmith	Miller
Brick maker	Parish constable
Butcher	Plumber and glazier
Carpenter	Postmaster
Cider retailer	Saddler
China and earthenware dealer	Roadman
Coal merchant	Shepherd
Dress maker	Stonemason
Farmers	Shoe maker
Farm bailiff	Tailor
Farm labourer	Traction engine driver
Fruit dealer	Wheelwright
Ironmonger	

Of these occupations agriculture was the most dangerous and grim accidents were not uncommon. Thomas Skarrat , the Kington draper, tells in his diary how in June 1877:

> A person at Eardisley, superintending a sawing-machine driven by steam by some misfortune came in contact with the saw and was cut so bad that he died.

Five years later, in September 1882:

> A fatal accident occurred in a harvest field at the *Upper House Farm* at Eardisley. Three men were engaged roping a waggon-load of wheat, one on the top, two on the ground. The rope broke causing the latter to fall on their backs; the other pitched on his head and died from the effects.

There were some strange combinations of occupation: in 1852 James Powell advertized himself as a grocer, draper, ironmonger, *and druggist*: Richard Llewellyn was a tailor and parish constable; and John Morgan sold both coal *and* beer.

The parish had its professionals, too:

> An absentee squire
>
> Clergymen: a Rector with four servants and a curate with none, taking in pupils to eke things out, and two nonconformist ministers
>
> A professionally qualified doctor, Octavius William Hoffman, MRCS, LSA. He succeeded John Augustus Davies, an apprenticed surgeon, who lived at *Bridge Cottage*.
>
> A midwife
>
> A nurse
>
> A bachelor schoolmaster
>
> Two retired army officers

From the reign of Elizabeth I until the Poor Law amendment Act of 1834, provision for the poor of the parish was administered by the Overseer of the Poor, chosen annually at the Easter vestry, and approved by the local magistrates. Once elected, it was obligatory for an Overseer to serve his year of office, and do so without salary or compensation for loss of earnings. He raised the funds needed for the relief he administered by levying a local rate.

The 1834 act introduced a new system whereby parishes were joined in Unions run by elected Boards of Guardians, each responsible for a work house, which often survived until the creation of the National Health Service in 1948. Eardisley which had previously had a small work house of its own, became part of the extensive Kington Union which built a large work house at Kingswood in 1837, capable of accommodating 100 inmates. It is now an old peoples' home, though its days are numbered.

To have to go to the work house was seen as a great humiliation, and in Eardisley one could subscribe to various charities and clubs which would reduce the likelihood of this happening. In 1866, for example, Eardisley had its Coal Charity; Wheat Charity; and Clothing Club. The Coal Charity was distributed a few days before Christmas and its funds were augmented by donations from the generous and wealthy. The Perry-Herricks and the Cokes, and the rectors were the principal benefactors. The 117 families who received coal in 1866 each paid 1s.3d. for their 5 cwts. allocation. Widows only paid 6d.. Local farmers hauled the coals from the station to recipients' homes and the turnpike gates at the *Tram Inn* and Willersley allowed the carts through without charging tolls.

The Wheat Charity was distributed on New Year's Day in the schoolroom. It was donated by the leading farmers of the parish, led by General Coke of Lemore with 10 bushels. In all 51 bushels were donated for distribution on 1st January 1867. The Clothing Club was run by the Vicar and Churchwardens, parishioners contributing a small regular subscription. In 1866 the club had 88 members, to whom the accumulated funds were distributed, with a half crown bonus, a reward for the subscribers' thriftiness. The bonus was provided by the Perry-Herrick family, Mr. Gibson-Watt of *Newport*, Almeley, and the vicar.

The coming to Eardisley first of the tramway, and then of the railway enlarged the lives of the parishioners immensely. The tramway did not take passengers, at least officially, but opened the resources of south Wales to the parish, especially in making coal more cheaply available.

In 1864 the Hereford, Hay, and Brecon Railway opened and thereby the world became Eardisley's oyster. The oyster was further enriched in 1874 when the line opened to Kington, and to New Radnor and Presteign in 1875. In 1885 the Hereford, Hay, and Brecon Railway was absorbed into the Midland Railway and through trains ran, at a somewhat leisurely pace, from Hereford to Swansea. Indeed, judicious amounts of shunting around Hereford enabled Midland trains to have the occasional through coach to the Great Western's Paddington itself.

And for those who had to change trains at Eardisley and endure lengthy waits for connections, there was a refreshment room at the station under personal the supervision of Miss Naomi Beaven, whose family were well known in the village. On occasion Miss Beaven's refreshments must have been positive life-safers. Of the four daily trains to Hereford, three came from Swansea, and only the early one started at Brecon. The complete journey from Swansea could involve as many as 24 stops, with 10 minute waits at Brecon and Three Cocks Junction for the convenience of nature, the trains having no corridors. It took such a train just under four hours to cover the 79 miles involved. Waiting for the GWR connection at Eardisley, many must have blessed Miss Beaven and her successors.

During the Second World War an American petrol, oil, and lubrication depot was established just outside the station by the junction with the then defunct Kington line. A siding was laid down, leading into what are now the saw mills. At the end of the war the removal of the surplus petrol and oil entailed, according to local memory, the services of at least nine trains of oil wagons. Eardisley was fortunate indeed to have escaped enemy air raids.

The last passenger train to use the station ran on December 31st 1962 and two years later the line was closed for goods traffic. In 1991 the station itself was dismantled and removed, lock stock and barrel, to Welshpool to be re-erected as the terminus building for the Welshpool and Llanfair Light Railway. Eardisley's large goods shed is now a private house.

Eardisley Parish Church

Walk 3: Almeley to Kinnersley

Leave the *Bells* and turn left down into Almeley village. Go past the *War Memorial*, *Church House*, and the *Parish Church*, all familiar sights by now to the careful readers of this book. Arriving at the turning to the left, for Sarnesfield, turn into it. A little way on, but before you arrive at the village school on the left, there is on the right a stile with a dog board. Use it, and, enjoying the splendid views of the Black Mountains in the distance, cross the field, following the hedge on your right. At the bottom of the field, cross the stile and footbridge, and carry on again to the bottom of the field, with the hedge still to your right. A double stile will now take you over a ditch, into a new field. Turn somewhat to your left and make for the stile opposite. Once over this, a look at the map shows that the footpaths soon divide. Take the right hand option, and continue across the field to the stile that awaits you. Continue across this next field, and another stile will take you into the lower part of a much larger field, subdivided with a new wire fence, which has a stile. Climb over and continue on ahead, with the hedge to your right until you arrive at an arrow-signed iron gate. Go through it and bear left, crossing a stile.

Following the direction of the yellow arrow cross a stile with a dog-gate, cross it and you will soon arrive at a wooden footbridge over a stream. Over it, with the path steadily rising, other tracks will filter in to your right, serving nearby houses, surrounded by trees and hedges, so that they can be barely seen. You will, however, see a timber framed house with brick in filling on your left, with its attendant farm buildings. The map shows that you could continue along what has become a something of a farm track, on to *Logaston Common Farm*. But don't: instead take the footpath going off the right, this takes you past *Little Logaston*. Enter a small paddock, continue on, leaving the paddock by crossing a stile and a bridge.

You are now in a large orchard and Bulmers would appreciate it if, in the interests of the quality of their cider, dogs were kept on the lead. Follow the fence on your left but before arriving at *Highfield Wood* in front of you, turn right down the hill and walk parallel to the rows of apple tress. You will again arrive at a fence bordering *Highfield Wood* on the left. Turn right here following the fence and you will see occasional badger gates. Ignore a gate into the wood, again, on your left. Leave the orchard by a stile and foot-bridge, and you are briefly in *Highfield Wood*. There soon comes, however another stile and bridge, giving access to an open field. With its tree-lined margin on your right, continue on to a footbridge and cross the associated stile. The public footpath is now behind us, and turning right we are once again amongst Bulmer's orchards.

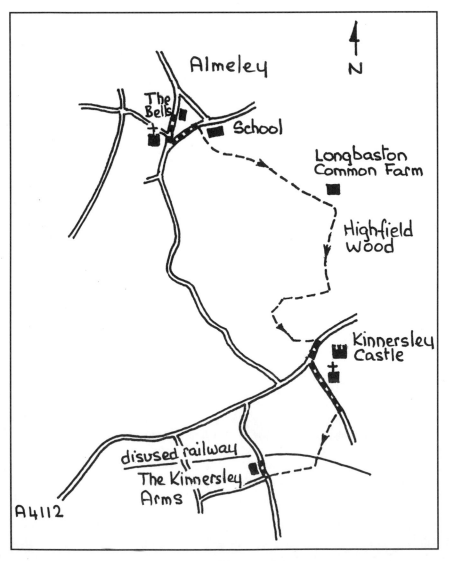

At present fruit trees obstruct the legal line of the path, which runs diagonally across both this field and the next one, and until they are removed, the following route should be followed.

With the fence on your right and a nursery of apple trees to your left, follow the course of the fence, until the path takes you away from it through the trees. When you arrive at a hedge with a stile through it, marked with an arrow, cross it. Then bear right and join a broad grassy way that will take you past a modern agricultural building. Here turn left and continue on until a fingerboard offers you the choice of going straight on down a lane, or of turning left. Turn left.

This new path through the orchard is broad and grassy. After a while, on the left, just off the track we have been following, there is a double stile. Cross it and, now out of Bulmer's orchards, following the arrow, cross the field with the hedge on the right. At the end of the field, and slightly to the left, a gate gives access to the A4112 Eardisley-Leominster road. It is usually busy and has to be crossed with care.

Safe on the side, turn right and walk along the grass verge, past the *Old Stables*, and the drive into *Kinnersley Castle*, then comes Kinnersley parish church, well worth a visit. The walk however does not end here, but at the *Kinnersley*. So turn left immediately beyond the church down a lane, sign posted as going to *Norton Wood*. It is very straight, pass *South Park*, a bungalow, on the left. Ignore the finger post on the right which would take you back to the A4112. A few yards further on, however, there is a stile to be crossed. It has an arrow on the step directing our path. A wire netting fence of modest height is ahead, but easy enough to get over. Further on, to the left, is a dead oak tree and just before it there is a little wooden footbridge, with an arrow on the handrail. Cross it and then turn diagonally to the right. Leaving the gully on your right, make for the stile and gate at the far left-hand corner of the field. This takes you on to the path, defined by trees and a hedge, of the dismantled railway line from Hereford to Brecon and beyond. A kissing gate and a wooden gate, now rather rare, are ahead. Follow the direction of the arrow and go straight on. At the next stile, follow the arrow across the open field. The *Kinnersley* can been seen, its roof peeping above the hedge. On reaching the Kinnersley-Letton road, cross the stile, ignore the lane ahead 'unsuitable for long vehicles' leading to the hamlet of Ailey. We will make its better acquaintance in another walk. Turn right and the *Kinnersley* awaits you on the left.

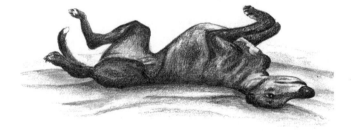

KINNERSLEY

The place-name Kinnersley commemorates another pre-Domesday clearing in the Herefordshire woodlands, this time that of Cynehearde. Domesday tells of Richard and Edric 'who could go where he would' and of '3 villagers and 6 smallholders with 4 ploughs.' The church in which Richard and Edric worshipped on Sundays and holy days has long been superseded, but its successor is in parts almost as ancient.

Dedicated to St James, it stands immediately west of the castle, which overlooks it, or rather looks down upon it, with a certain degree of *hauteur*. The churchyard is immaculately groomed and in 1993 was the best kept in Herefordshire. One realises one is entering a world apart, for at the churchyard gate there were garden plants for sale, all unattended, and we are all trusted. This sense is enhanced by the high brick walls, which separate the churchyard from the adjoining grounds of Kinnersley Castle.

The dedication to St James the Greater, the patron of pilgrims, was particularly popular in Herefordshire in the twelfth century, and St James' shrine at Compostella was the object of their long and dangerous journey. One of these Herefordshire pilgrims was Oliver de Merlinmond, who built a church at Shobdon. Others who went to Compostella from Herefordshire were stone-masons and attention has been drawn to striking similarities between details in the designs of sculpture in the churches at Eardisley, Canon Frome, and Kilpeck and the church of Santiago Compostella. There are also similarities between the work of the Herefordshire school of sculpture and the ornament to be seen on some of the doorways of the church at Parthenay-le-Vieux, some 200 miles south-east of Paris. Though there are no examples of this artistic relationship to be seen at Kinnersley, it is not an impossible hypothesis that its dedication to St James belongs to the 12th century.

But be this as it may, the oldest part of the church faces us as we come up the churchyard path. It is the large Norman doorway in the west wall of the nave, which has since been blocked up. Why? The great west door of a church had liturgical importance, so why dispose of it? One possible explanation lies in human vanity. A large memorial to an 18th century worthy occupies this prime space on the interior of the west wall, and all would see it, as they returned from the altar after making their communion, or as they left the church.

The projecting string course above this doorway is also Norman, and was later interrupted during the perpendicular period by the insertion of a large west window. The *savants* of the Cambrian Archaeological Association, when they inspected the church in 1863, thought this window to be 'very singular' and 'remarkable for its length and narrowness'. Perhaps what they were saying in academic terms was that its proportions were not very good.

The nave and the north and south aisles, though added later, are all under one stone tiled roof, and there are no clerestories. Most of the present church, however, was built c.1300. Later in the 14th century the stone tiled timber porch, its bargeboards enriched with tracery, was added to protect the south door, and the 15th century saw the renewal of the four bays of the south arcade. Their pillars, elegant and slim, and their lofty arches, stand in contrast with their stouter, sturdier counterparts of the opposite north aisle. At the same time a turret was built at the east end of this south arcade to accommodate a stairway giving access to the rood loft over the screen separating chancel and nave.

For Pevsner the most impressive feature of the church, is its mighty almost detached tower, battled and defensive, set at the northern end of the west side of the church, with its sheer outline and its saddleback roof. The Cambrians, too, saw it as 'a handsome well-proportioned structure surmounted with a plain saddle-back roof, or rather a common gable'. They thought the date of the tower is probably of the thirteenth century, and were irritated by what was in 1863 a modern doorway, which interfered with the small window above it. The arch and supporting shafts of this offending door, were dismissed as 'modem clumsy work, in imitation of Early English'.

One who enjoyed and served this church in its pre-reformation guise, was *Dominus* William Leviot. He was rector here and died in 1421. He is commemorated, in alb and amice, on the north wall of the chancel by a brass and a Latin inscription. The use of the term *Dominus* in Medieval Latin implies that he was a Bachelor of Arts.

The Reformation was accepted reluctantly by many in Herefordshire and the Vaughans who had acquired the advowson of the church and ownership of the castle towards the end of the 16th century were loyal to their Catholicism. With this in mind it was perhaps the Commonwealth rather than the Reformation which saw the loss of the chancel screen, with the exception of its decorated base, and rood, and probably the stained glass which may have adorned the large three-light east window of the chancel. The stone altar of sacrifice was replace by a wooden Jacobean table of communion. But there were gains too and the reredos, choir stalls, and pulpit all contain interesting post Reformation woodwork. The Cambrians thought the oak reredos something of a curiosity, and their hope that it would 'be most carefully preserved' has been fulfilled. It may have originated as a domestic overmantle to a fireplace. They were less certain about the carvings on the pulpit, of 'tolerable execution, though not of very ecclesiastical character'. Another domestic looking 17th century table serves the Lady Chapel.

The Cambrians also noted on the north side of the chancel 'a huge monument of the Smallmans' and thought it 'a good specimen of such a class'. Pevsner was rather more enthusiastic. Carved in alabaster and marble, and enriched with trumpet blowing cherubs, it commemorates the death of Francis Smallman of Kinnersley Castle in 1633. Pevsner considered it 'a very fine piece. . . . all very lively and not at all stiff'. Smallman was Sheriff of Herefordshire in 1614 and MP for Leominster 1620-22. He was twice married, and his second wife, Susan, was also twice married, a fact which reflects the mortality, rather than the divorce rate, of the period. His eldest son, another Francis, married Katharine Coningsby, daughter of Sir Thomas Coningsby who was prominent in the affairs of Herefordshire and the Marches, and is remembered in Hereford by the Coningsby Hospital in Widemarsh Street, founded in 1614 for superannuated soldiers and servants.

Kinnersley Castle

In the process of time the Smallmans of Kinnersley Castle gave way to the Morgans of Kinnersley Castle, and they, too, have their memorials in the church, a mark of 18th century conspicuous consumption. On the west wall of the nave another large monument commemorates Lady Ann Morgan who died in 1764. Her husband, Sir John Morgan, Bart, died in 1767 and was the last of the line. They married in 1729, Ann being a daughter of Sir Jacob Jacobsen, of Walthamstow, Essex. Her brother, Theodore Jacobsen, FRS, FSA, d. 1772, was the architect of the Foundling Hospital. The monument is the work of Nicholas Read, d. 1787, pupil of Roubiliac 'whose extravagant style he imitated'.

At the east end of the north aisle there is another reminder of human mortality and the sudden death from which the Prayer Book Litany seeks our deliverance. It is a memorial to John Parkinson who died in 1804 at Winchester College, aged 16. Pevsner approved of this piece of funerary art:

> The monument has a very fine roundel with a mourning female
> figure at the foot. The lettering is good and restrained too.

A contemporary at Winchester of John Parkinson was John Eagles, 1783-1855. After Winchester, Eagles trained as a landscape artist before going up to Oxford to prepare for ordination. He was assistant curate for a while to Sydney Smith, the clerical wit, but later served Kinnersley, 'for a friend', it is said, presumably the incumbent. He retired from clerical life in 1841 but continued to enjoy a reputation as a literary critic.

The limited stained glass in the church is more interesting as biography than art. The east window in the chancel depicts the Last Supper and the Resurrection. It is in memory of the Revd John Clutton, MA, DD, who died, full of years, in 1851. He was a native of Birmingham and went up to St John's College, Oxford in 1778, at the age of 18 and graduated in succession as BA, MA, BD, and DD. He inherited Kinnersley castle and lived a none too strenuous life as a prebendary of Hereford cathedral. His eldest son, another John, followed in his father's footsteps, entering Worcester College, Oxford in 1822. After taking his BA and MA he was installed at Hereford cathedral as Prebendary of Norton in 1831 and enjoyed its revenues until his death in 1885, so father and son together influenced the cathedral's affairs for twenty years. John Clutton Junior's younger brother, Thomas Clutton, went up to New College, Oxford in 1825 and was a Fellow of the college for 35 years.

A stained glass window in the north wall of the sanctuary commemorates the splendidly named Isabella Horatia, the wife of the then rector, the Revd

Leonard Clarke, MA, and who died in 1847. Leonard, educated at Brasenose College, Oxford, was presented to the living by his father, John Altham Clarke, Senior, of Kinnersley castle in 1844, and remained as incumbent until 1861. His father married the daughter of Leonard Parkinson, whose son, it will be remembered, has a sad memorial in the north aisle. Perhaps Clarke named *his* second son Leonard as a gesture to his father-in-law.

Leonard Clarke's elder brother, John Altham Clarke, Junior, also educated at Brasenose, succeeded his father in 1862. Twenty years later he and his wife were living stylishly, with the assistance of a cook, lady's maid, housemaid, kitchen maid, a page boy, and governess, in Gloucestershire at the Manor House, Frocester, near Stroud.

Four years after the visit of the Cambrians to Kinnersley in 1863, the church was restored by Thomas Nicholson, the diocesan architect. This visit of the Cambrians *before* this restoration enables Nicholson to be given credit which he has long been denied. The account of their visit in *Archaeologia Cambrensis,* for example, shows that both the reredos and pulpit were in the church in 1863. Likewise, since Nicholson preserved these furnishings, which may well have been of secular origin, it is unlikely that he would have removed the rood screen, as has been suggested elsewhere. This was genuinely ecclesiastical and must therefore have been dismantled beforehand, probably during the Commonwealth if it survived the Reformation.

Nicholson worked at Kinnersley in conjunction with the incumbent, the Revd Francis Fenwick Reavely, whose father Thomas Reavely, 1789-1872, a native of Northumberland, was at the time patron of the living and master of Kinnersley castle. Educated at Trinity College, Cambridge where he graduated as a Student in Civil Law in 1854, Francis Reavely was made deacon the same year at Lincoln cathedral. Four years later he was ordained priest and presented to Kinnersley. He married Fanny Abby, the daughter of the Revd William Domville, MA, rector of nearby Winforton.

Nicholson rebuilt the chancel arch and removed the grotesques on either side mentioned by the Cambrians. He also installed an organ, built by Bevington of London. It was paid for by Mrs Reavely, the rector's wife, in memory of her sister, Miss Emily Domville of Winforton. The vestry was added to the north side of the chancel at the same time and the church was reseated with the present pews. The floor tiles and the two large chandeliers hanging in the nave probably belong to the same period, but the largest part of the restoration was probably the installation of uniform sets of flat headed windows, which characterise both the south and north aisles and make the church so light. The total cost of it all was £1,500 and the church was reopened for public worship on Easter Sunday 1869. The tower was restored in 1871, the work being paid for by the churchwarden, Col Bridgford of Upper Newton.

Robert Bridgford, 1836-1905, was a Lieutenant Colonel in the Herefordshire Volunteers and land agent, perhaps to the Reavelys. A Lancastrian by birth, he had not been long settled at Newton in 1871, but he was to become a JP, Deputy Lieutenant, and first a Companion, and then a Knight of the Order of the Bath. One of his several sons, Robert James Bridgford, 1869-1954, had a distinguished military career. Prepared for Charterhouse by the Curate of Eardisley, the Revd Donald Cameron, MA, he joined the King's Light Infantry in 1889. He served in South Africa 1899-1900, and his courage in the defence of Ladysmith was mentioned in dispatches and he was in consequence awarded the DSO. By the time of the Great War, 1914-18, in which he was wounded and again mentioned in dispatches, he was a Major General. He retired in 1922 and made his home at Staunton-on-Arrow. The immediate connection of the Bridgfords with Kinnersley seems to have ended by 1881 when WR Dewing lived at Newton, describing himself as a gentleman farmer, with 300 acres to prove it. His family home was in Norfolk at Carbrooke Hall near Thetford.

But to return to the Reavelys and Kinnersley church. In 1872, Thomas Reavely died, and his eldest son, Thomas II, 1829-1904, inherited Kinnersley Castle. In 1850 he married a German wife, Johanna Maria Wilhelmina Stiefvater of Hamburg and their first child, Thomas George Wood Reavely, was born in Hamburg in 1852. Soon after their arrival in Kinnersley in 1872 the rector resigned and moved to another family living, that of West Lexham in Norfolk. Here he managed to combine his parochial duties with a chaplaincy to the English residents at Pozznozi in Italy. Mrs Reavely died in 1881 and in 1883 Francis Reavely married a middle-aged French spinster, Bertha Rensch, then of Charlton Kings, near Cheltenham.

Thomas Reavely II, 1829-1904, was a pillar of the establishment. A Justice of the Peace, Deputy Lieutenant, he was High Sheriff of Herefordshire in 1867 and had a town house in Portman Street. He broke with the tradition of treating the living as a family asset and his choice of incumbent for Kinnersley was the Revd Frederick Andrews, BA. Educated at St John's College, Cambridge, he graduated in 1866 and was made deacon that year by the Bishop of Winchester, and started his working life as a schoolmaster. Then, after curacies in Surrey at East Molesey and Thames Ditton, he came to Kinnersley in 1873 as a young married man of 29.

Some saw the rectory in which Mr and Mrs Andrews made their home as a substantial stone residence, delightfully situated near the castle, surrounded by extensive ornamental grounds, and commanding some most beautiful and extensive prospects. Others described it simply as 'a neat cottage residence'. You can judge for yourself which description is the more accurate, because, though no longer a rectory, the house still stands, opposite the church, on the other side of the A4112 to Eardisley. By 1881 it was occupied by Mr and Mrs Andrews, their five children, and cook, housemaid, and nurse, so perhaps it was rather more than just a cottage residence.

A year before the arrival of Frederick Andrews, Minna Frances Henrietta, daughter of Thomas Reaveley II, aged 19 married the architect George Frederick Bodley, 1827-1907, 26 years her senior. Bodley's connection with Herefordshire began in 1854 when he designed the parish church at Longrove. He was at Canon Frome in 1860, at Kingsland in 1866, and at Lyonshall in 1872 and as the *Dictionary of National Biography* puts it:

> Bodley fills an important position in the history of English ecclesiastical architecture. If Pugin, Scott and Street were the pioneers whose work went hand in hand with the Oxford movement in its early days, Bodley is their counterpart in the last quarter of the nineteenth century. Between 1870 and 1880 he and his partner [Thomas Garner] stood alone as experts in the propriety of internal church decoration, and thence to the end of his life Bodley was justly looked upon as combining ecclesiological knowledge with sound taste (especially in colour decoration) to a degree which few rivals could approach.

He was a frequent enough visitor to Kinnersley to have designed wallpaper for use in the castle, and for the rector to have made his acquaintance. In 1887 he drew up a scheme of decoration for the church. This event is recorded in Latin by a framed illuminated notice, resting on the sill of the window in the north wall of the chancel. However, though Andrews admired Bodley's aesthetics and scholarship, it is not so certain that he shared his churchmanship. In the north aisle there hang two boards whereon are painted, in accordance with the canons of 1602, the Ten Commandments and the Lord's Prayer, though space did not allow room for the Creed, which should also have been displayed. They are in the same medieval script as is used elsewhere in the church, and are largely illegible to the untrained eye. This defeats the intention of the 1604 canons, which was that these fundamental Christian statements should be easily read and learned by the congregations which saw them hanging either side of the altar, their prescribed position.

Tractarians, however, like Bodley, removed these texts in their church restorations as not being in accordance with the recommended practice of the Ecclesiological Society, established to give Victorian restorers guidance on what was then believed to be both sound theology and good taste. Andrews must have thought otherwise.

Pevsner thought Bodley's scheme of decoration for the nave and chancel 'exceedingly pretty'. And so it is, with its use of reds, greens, blues, gold and black, intermingled with Latin texts, the result is appropriately medieval. The reredos was enriched at the expense of Col Robert Bridgford of Newton, and the Reavely organ sold and a new one, by Wordsworth and Maskell, erected in memory of the Revd John Clutton II. It was larger than its predecessor, and was decorated according to Bodlean principles. But it sits uncomfortably in the chancel, being too large for its position, detracting from the liturgical emphasis upon the altar. The modern electric organ blower actually intrudes into the sanctuary and thereby reduces the stretch of the altar rails, and concealing the organist behind a curtain makes one wonder what arcane activity is actually involved in accompanying a service. In 1888 the present instrument cost £240 and it was recently restored for £15,000.

Relations between the Reavelys and Frederick Andrews and his wife were close. Thomas Reavely III was born in 1852 at Hamburg. Educated at Harrow and Cambridge, he continued the German connection by studying at the University of Jena where he graduated as a DCL in 1877. He became a barrister and lived at Kinnersley. His full name was Thomas George *Wood* Reavely and when another son was born to Mr and Mrs Andrews in 1878, he was christened Robert *Wood* Andrews.

Bodley was last professionally in Herefordshire in 1906-6 supervising the building at Hom Green, the Church of the Paraclete, and when he died in 1907 at the age of 80, he was buried in Kinnersley churchyard. His grave is near those of the Reavely family, the Bridgfords, and that of Frederick Andrews who died in 1920, having been rector for 47 rears. They all lie on the west side of the church under the shadow of a gigantic Celtic High Cross of Ahenny. This looks strangely alien in the pastoral setting of Herefordshire.

Though at present unringable the church has four bells, of the seventeenth and eighteenth centuries. The earliest was cast by Henry Farmer, of Gloucester in 1618, and bears the name of Francis Smallman as its donor. John Greene, of Worcester, cast the heaviest of the four in 1634, weighing seven and a half hundred weights. The treble was cast by Henry Clibury, of

Wellington, in Shropshire in 1671, and the fourth at the famous Chepstow foundry of William Evans in 1760. They were re-hung in 1868, but as a peal they would have sounded very curious for they are not tuned to any recognizable scale. Unfortunately, their frame and fittings are no longer serviceable.

The tower also houses the mechanism of the clock, the face of which on the west wall faces the congregation coming into the churchyard to remind them they are late. It was given in 1945 by Lord and Lady Brocket as a thank-offering. Lord Brocket, 1904-1967, educated at Eton and Oxford, was an MP briefly before succeeding to the title in 1934. He acquired Kinnersley castle in 1940 and sold it in 1945.

To Pevsner *Kinnersley* castle appeared 'towering, commanding, and forbidding behind the church', but it did not impress the Cambrians of 1863:

> Of the original castle, on the site of which stands a spacious structure of the time of James the First, no traces could be discovered beyond one or two portions of a plinth in the cellars, which may be of the fifteenth century, and may be later. The view from the top of the tower, which contains the staircase, however, made amends for the lack of architectural interest below.

It is Elizabethan, built by Roger Vaughan between c.1585 and 1601, and appears so in most of its features, but its great embattled tower, five floors high, shows it was once a true castle. In 1250 Hugh de Kinnersley was Sheriff of Herefordshire and in 1307 Hugh de Kinnersley was MP for the shire. A Richard de Kinnersley appears in 1316 and in 1340 Sir Richard de la Bere, Lord of the Manor, obtained a license to hold a market and a fair at Kinnersley. Six years later he fought with distinction at the battle of Crecy in 1346: perhaps some of the Welsh bowmen who made this so signal a victory, accompanied him from Kinnersley. In 1353 he was MP for Herefordshire. All these lived in this earlier castle.

It was Roger Vaughan, eldest son of Roger Vaughan of Clyro, a member of the ubiquitous Vaughan family, who rebuilt Kinnersley castle c. 1585-90. He was active in the affairs of Breconshire and Radnorshire, serving as Sheriff for both, and he was MP for Radnorshire 1572-83. He was, too, an intimate friend of Sir Gelly Meyrick of Gladestry, executed for his loyalty to Essex in 1601. It was also in 1601 that Vaughan himself, living now at Kinnersley, was involved in a case of poisoning.

He rebuilt the castle in an L-shape and some of the medieval masonry may have survived in the tower. It was all done in the latest architectural fashion, and this seems to have surprised Pevsner who thought the building had several 'enjoyable Elizabethan features'. In particular he noted:

> The stepped brick gables on a stone house and a veneer in front of actual stone gables are specially interesting, as they were no doubt at the moment fashionable, though quite unusual in Herefordshire.

But this should not surprise us, the Vaughans were Welsh-speaking, as was Queen Elizabeth I, and one of their kinswomen was a Lady of the Bedchamber. This was Margaret Vaughan of Hergest Court, near Kington, the second wife of Sir John Hawkins, and foundress of the school in Kington which now bears her name. Several of the Vaughans were educated in one of the Inns of Court, in the 16th century an alternative to Oxford and Cambridge. Hergest Court and Bredwardine were places where the Welsh bards were always welcome. So it is no surprise that Roger Vaughan should have a taste for fashion in deciding the appearance of his mansion.

Roger Vaughan died in 1607, and his son John, who was Sheriff for Radnorshire that year, made his home at Kinnersley and the fire place in the drawing room bears his crest. He married Joan, heiress of Richard Baynham of Aston Ingham, Herefordshire, and it was she, John Vaughan presumably being dead, who sold the castle in 1618 to Francis Smallman.

Pevsner described the castle warmly, and there is a full illustrated account of its architecture in the third volume of the Royal Commission on Historical Monuments in England's *Inventory of the Historical Monuments in Herefordshire*. There is also a very informative page on the website:

http://www.kinnersley.com/castle/.

Then after various vicissitudes of fortune the castle passed by marriage to Thomas Clutton of Pensax, Worcestershire, who, in 1801 sold it to Leonard Parkinson whose memorial in the church to his sixteen- year old son moves the heart. In 1812 Parkinson's daughter married John Altham Graham Clarke, Senior, of Newcastle upon Tyne. He sold it in the 1850s to another Northumbrian, Thomas Reavely, Senior, and it remained in Reavely hands until 1940. A picture of Kinnersley castle as a scene of English country life amongst the gentry in the late 19th century is painted by Thomas Reavely, Junior's invitation to the Herefordshire Bow Meeting to come to Kinnersley in August 1890 for one of its archery gatherings. But it was not always so, and when the census was taken in 1881, the castle was empty, except for Mary Pugh, the 71 year-old housekeeper.

When the shadow of war fell upon Herefordshire in 1914 the castle was used as a hospital for Belgians, and the Reavelys seem not to have lived there again, but leased the property to a series of tenants. In 1954 it was purchased by Mr H Garatt-Adams, and after a some years as home for the elderly, it is now what is described as 'a family enterprise'. The castle and the gardens can be visited from time to time by prior arrangement.

Exploring the byways of nautical history one comes across the fact that in April 1817 one of His Majesty's troop transports, the *Kinnersley Castle,* in company with the *Pomona* and *Hussdren,* sailed from Portsmouth for Cowes 'to take detachments of regiments from thence to North America. In 1819 the *Kinnersley Castle* was engaged in transporting the 13th Regiment and Rifle Brigade, their baggage, the staff horses, the regimental wives and children from Plymouth to Leith. *The Times* reported that the voyage was not accomplished without difficulty. Because of the wind, blowing strong from the eastward, the vessel 'was able to make but little progress'.

The careers of army transports at this period are difficult to chronicle, because shortly after the conclusion of the Napoleonic Wars the Board of Commissioners for Transport was wound up, and its powers transferred to the Admiralty. In consequence of this, the status of the *Kinnersley Castle* became similar to that of the modern Fleet Auxiliary and there would have been no need for her to be registered at Lloyds, whose register is normally an invaluable source of shipping information.

In 1820 Sir Gregor Macgregor, a Scottish adventurer, obtained in Central America a tract of fertile land amongst the Poyais Indians. He encouraged trade, established schools, and projected a bank, and established a small army. He also attempted to introduce Scottish immigrants to his settlement, and some of these sailed to Poyais in the *Kinnersley Castle.* Sadly the venture was not a success and in Edinburgh in 1820 there was published the book *A particular account of the fate of the emigrants who sailed from Leith for Poyais in the Kinnersley Castle, with the names ... of 42 passengers, who have died, etc.*

No more is heard of the *Kinnersley Castle* until February 1833, when, no longer a transport, she became the subject of a lawsuit in the Admiralty Division of the High Court. The vessel had sailed from Waterford to Pugwash in Nova Scotia and on her return journey to Liverpool ran aground off Picton Island. The master deserted his ship and the officer who assumed control of the vessel in his place took out a bond of *bottomry,* a form of maritime mortgage, to pay for the salvage of the vessel. Meanwhile the ship's owner had gone bankrupt, and the question for judgement was whether the money had been really lent on the security of the ship and its cargo, or on the credit of the underwriters. The judge pronounced the question to be 'a rather nice one', and that he should take time to consider his judgement. When he delivered it he found that the money had been lent on the security of the underwriters.

But to return to the history of Kinnersley itself. Its railway station was almost opposite the *Kinnersley Arms,* and the parish's entry into the railway age began with John Altham Graham Clarke, Senior, of Kinnersley castle. Though described simply as a farmer in an 1852 directory, Clarke was in fact a considerable landowner who believed in railways. In 1818 he was one of the original proprietors of the Kington Tramway in which he invested £200. In 1845 he was an advocate of the proposed *Radnorshire, Aberystwith and Welsh Midland Junction Railway.* This remarkable example of railway mania was going to start on its unfulfilled route to Cardigan Bay in one direction and to Hereford in the other, here in the parish of Kinnersley at the *Parks,* then part of Clarke's Kinnersley estate.

It was not as fanciful as it may now seem that a main line railway should originate in the parish of Kinnersley, population 356, some twenty years before the Hereford, Hay, and Brecon Railway passed that way. In the same year, 1845, Richard Parry, the Kington historian, recorded that:

> Great efforts are now being made to form a new railway, to commence near the basin of the Worcester and Birmingham canal and the river Severn, in the parish of St Peter the Great, in the city of Worcester; and thence be carried by a viaduct across the Teme to Tenbury, thence to Wofferton *(sic)* cross, near Ludlow, and to Leominster and by the Vale of Arrow to Monkland, thence to Luntley, Broxwood, Woonton, Almeley and Eardisley.

It was then to follow the Wye through Clyro and Glasbury, and from there to make its way through Talgarth to Llanfihangel Talyllyn and Merthyr Tydfil, in all eighty miles of main line. The required capital of £1,500,000 could not be raised and no more was heard of this proposed railway, though the Kington banker and lawyer, Richard Banks, continued to regret its failure for many years. But had it materialised, passing through the parishes of Kinnersley and Eardisley *en route* for Merthyr Tydfil, a junction with the line to Aberystwyth would have presented no problems.

The railway age came to Kinnersley in earnest in 1864 when the Hereford, Hay and Brecon Railway opened its line from Hereford to Hay-on-Wye. Ironically when *The Parks* was up for sale in 1880, one of its advertized selling points was that it was but a mile from Kinnersley station on the Hereford, Hay and Brecon Railway. In 1885 it was absorbed into the Midland Railway and through trains ran, at a somewhat leisurely pace, from Hereford to Swansea. Kilvert was one, when he was rector of Bredwardine, who frequently took the train from Kinnersley. The last passenger train to use the station ran on December 31st 1962 and two years later the line was closed for goods traffic. The *Kinnersley* was once known as *Station Hotel.* Before that it was the *Belle Vue,* which in 1881 had an 80 year old licensee: Alfred Yates, a signal man, lived nearby at *Belle Vue Cottage.* Indeed, according to the 1881 census, the railway offered several Kinnersley men employment. William Pember was a plate-layer, John Bruce who lodged at the *Smithy* was a railway porter, and Charles Wilkes was a railway labourer. There was a station master too, and in 1905 his wife died, aged 45, and was buried in the churchyard. Robert Bennett, a waggoner, lived at *Railway Cottage.*

In 1902 Arthur Thomas was a blacksmith and contractor, living 'near the station', and Thomas Lewis, a builder and contractor, was also a coal, coke, lime, and manure merchant, besides being 'agent for Swift, Humber, Raleigh, Singer, and other best cycle makers'. John Taylor, was an agent for the Old Radnor Company Ltd, which brought its lime to Kinnersley by rail and had a depot at the station. In 1902 James Turner of the *Belle Vue Hotel,* was an agent for the rival Breconshire Coal and Lime Company, Ltd., which also had a depot at the railway station. There was, too, James Williams of the *Old School House* who was another coal agent, dependant upon the railway for his supplies. Even in 1945 there were comprehensive services, which only the railway could offer a rural community. Thus, when Lord Brocket left Kinnersley that year and returned to Brocket Hall, near Hatfield in Hertfordshire, a special train took him, lock, stock, and barrel, animals and all.

A hundred and thirty years ago alternative resorts of refreshment to the *Belle Vue* were offered by the *Masons' Arms,* at Ailey, kept by Charles Evans, a 26 year old bachelor, and the *New Inn,* presided over by John Watkins, a carpenter. Occupations relating to timber were well represented in the parish, and there were several sawyers and wheelwrights. There were farm bailiffs, too, as well as numerous farm labourers, for agriculture was still very labour intensive. There was, too, a cordwinder, a professional charwoman, a dress-maker, a couple of blacksmiths, and Herbert Bromley, who described

himself as a 'Prize Fowl Breeder'. The roads were being taken more seriously, and the parish had two road-men, the wife of one was a laundress. In
1881 the new tenants of the Parks farm, shorn of its 'short horn and
Hereford cattle and grand and powerful cart horses' had John Price, a blacksmith, as a lodger. Lastly, there was a National School for the education of
the village children. In 1881 it was presided over by Miss Trott, a young lady
of 22, who lived at the School House, with her mother and various relations.
In 1902 her successor was Miss M Troughton, who sounds more formidable.

———————————

Walk 4: Kinnersley to Bredwardine

This walk has the great advantage that though it is of reasonable length, much of it is along a bridle path, which means there are very few stiles to carry the dog over. Gabby was very pleased to be spared that indignity. It is also, in comparison with the other walks, very flat.

Leave the *Kinnersley*, and turn right down the road towards Letton. In a short distance you will see two sign posts on the left-hand side of the road. One directs you to Lower Ailey Farm on the other side of the road, and the other one points out our route down a grassy lane, which leaves the road on the left-hand side. Soon there will be an orchard to the right, pasture to the left, and a distant view of Ladylift hill ahead.

We were on the threshold of autumn when we did this walk, and there was an equinoctial gale blowing. We made our way through a constant flurry of falling leaves from the fine oaks along the right-hand side of the lane. Pass the farm on your right and do not be dismayed by the notice to beware of the Border collie living there. After a new redbrick house and then a much older house on the left the lane becomes more a track than a lane. Arriving at a T-junction, turn right, along what is still officially a bridle path. It now runs alongside the bed of the disused Hereford, Hay, and Brecon railway. The path is now wooded on both sides, and the effect is rather pleasant and arcadian.

Pass a farm on the right, where the geese were getting fat, unaware of their Christmas destiny. The path is now very grassy and with a few ruts from the occasional tractor. Continue until two gates confront you: take the one to the right and so part company with the bed of the old railway track. This is still a bridle path, taking you through Herefordshire's pastoral scenery at its best, an orchard on the right, cattle in the meadow on the left.

Through the gate ahead and carry along the lane until it comes to an end and you are confronted by two more gates. Take the left-most gate and cross a little stream with rushes growing by it, using the bridge. One is reminded of Mrs Alexander's children's hymn *All things bright and beautiful*, which speaks of

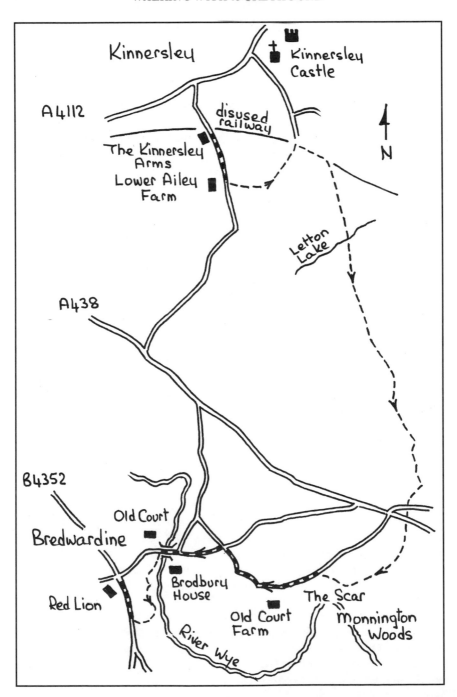

> The tall tress in the greenwood,
> The meadows for our play,
> The rushes by the water,
> To gather every day.

Victorian children in the country did this, gathering the rushes to cover the earthen floors of the small comfortless hovels in which they had to live. These have long since disappeared, and the small timber framed cottages which have survived hereabouts were of the relatively prosperous who did not need the handouts of food, money, and clothing provided for the parishioners of Letton, Staunton, and Bredwardine by the local Jarvis Charity.

We are crossing Letton Lake which, before the days of professional drainage schemes, flooded each year, when the courses of the streams making their way across these fields to the Wye were unable to cope with the seasonal surge of water. The meadows are still rather marshy in places.

Continue across the field, following the narrow path worn by the sheep. It seems to meander somewhat, but a glance at the map shows the route of the path is almost Roman in its sense of undeviating direction. Who used these bridle paths in the past? The possession of a horse was a status symbol, and one can imagine the squire, the parson, the doctor, as well as the farmer, all on horseback, using these paths. Sir George Cornewall Lewis, Liberal MP for Herefordshire 1847-52, tells in his diaries how, when he came to defend his seat in 1852, he was canvassing the scattered villages and hamlets of the constituency, travelling on horseback, often for eight or nine hours a day. The weather was bad, and he fell off his horse more than once. And all to no purpose, for in his diary he admits he met with but 'indifferent success', and he lost the seat. In contrast the modern riders using these bridle paths do so for pleasure and recreation, and find their way into Betjemanesque poetry

Ladylift is now on the left in the distance and Bredwardine hill on our right. Arriving at another stream, cross by the bridge and go through the gate beyond, bearing a request that we remember to close it. Continue across the field in the same direction as you have come. Through the next gate and Tin Hill is on the right. Another gate and over another stream, with its bank-side rushes, and follow the course of the sheep track as it seems to continue to meander across the field. Through the next gate, still follow the narrow sheep track, bearing slightly to the left. Then comes another little concrete bridge and another field. This leads to a copse, entered by an iron gate, with a directing sign, and go on into the lane ahead.

We are now in *Little London* and this takes us back to the days of the drovers. There was a flourishing cattle trade in the mid-thirteenth century and by the mid-seventeenth century the export of Welsh black store cattle to English towns and cities was one of the primary sources of Welsh revenue. Even ducks and geese made the journey, their feet being dipped in tar. Some of the journeys undertaken by the drovers were prodigious, taking them, far beyond London, to destinations in Kent, Surrey, and Sussex. Such was the importance of the trade that during the Civil War hostilities were temporarily suspended to allow safe passage of cattle being driven to London's Smithfield and elsewhere.

The droves varied in size between a hundred and four hundred head of cattle, which were shod and were often re-shod on the journey. This gave welcome work to blacksmiths on the way. The drovers left their mark in the names of some of the local fields wherein they pastured their flocks and herds on the way. This is the explanation of the unlikely *Little London*. The introduction of tollgates made long journeys from Wales very expensive and the drovers tried to avoid paying tolls by travelling cross-country. Once at their destinations, and their cattle sold, they carried out commissions for the farmers whose fields they had used on their journey. The drovers handled large sums of money in their transactions of behalf of the farmers whose cattle they drove and some believe they had some part in the development of country banking. With the advent of the railways, however, in the mid-nineteenth century, the drovers took advantage of the trains, and disappeared from the rural scene.

So much for *Little London*. The lane takes us past the back of a white house on the right, pass *Cherry Tree Cottage*, a black and white house, *Box Tree Cottage* on the left, *Walnut Cottage*, its Michaelmas daisies and hollyhocks still in flower. A sign-posted public footpath then crosses our bridle path. There is a stone and timber framed cottage on the left, a signed stile through the hedge on the right, a house on the left, *The Ark*, perhaps so named on account of its curious profile, a couple of bungalows, and a timber framed cottage, *The Rowles*. These were all on the left-hand side of the path.

We are now in the parish of Staunton-on-Wye, on the outskirts of the village. Herefordshire has two Stauntons, on Wye and on Arrow, and they stand out as being stone built settlements in a largely wooded and timber framed environment. The track has now become a surfaced lane. On the right one arrives at a public footpath sign. Turn down this track and leave the lane. A gate across the path and a yellow arrow will soon direct you through a farmyard. Bear left past the farm, another sign on a stile takes us past a barn, through a gate on the right, where there is another sign. There is a timber-framed farmhouse set back to the right, and a little pond to the left, and then go through a gate with another yellow arrow. In a field on your right you will see a sad piece of industrial archaeology in the form of a yellow rusting Morris Minor van, in its final death throes. Cross a lane, which to the right, takes you to the A438 a short distance away, and into Staunton village by turning to the left. Follow the yellow arrow and go through a gate, yet another timber framed cottage being on the other side of the hedge. Go ahead, with the hedge to your right, and you will soon come to a stile, which seems to take you into the garden of house called *Springfield*. Undeterred, cross the stile [Gabby's first indignity for the whole walk], turn immediately to your left and you will see the busy A438 ahead of you.

Cross the A438 and a little to your right there is a stile. Cross this and follow the left margin of the field. Go through a low wooden gate, and cross the next field to an arrowed stile, with a ditch before it. Continue with the hedge on your right to the next field, with the hedge still on the right. Once through the gate, the footpath becomes a bridle path.

This bridle path will take us to the *Scar* and the Ordnance Survey Map shows we have joined the *Wye Valley Walk*. The term *scar*, denoting a lofty, steep face of rock upon a mountainside, or a precipice or cliff, is more characteristic of Derbyshire than Herefordshire, but it is appropriate enough here. Through the trees, to your left, the Wye flows placidly below you, and though this is not Tintern Abbey, Wordsworth's lines come to mind:

> O sylvan Wye! Thou wanderer thro' the woods,
> How oft has my spirit turned to thee!

An opening to your left gives access to *Monnington Woods,* part of the Garnons Estate, and a well displayed notice tells the public they are welcome to walk in these woods from March 1st to August 1st.

The footpath has become more like a lane, going downhill, and still wooded with more sumptuous views to the left.

We now filter into a surfaced lane from the right. It has come from Handmore Cross at Staunton on the A438 which we crossed earlier. We are now in the parish of Brobury, which is so small in size and population, that it is little more than a name. Like so many other local place-names, it occurs in Domesday, and commemorates 'the defended place on the stream', the stream being the Wye.

Continue along this lane, ignore the turning to your left for *Old Court Farm*, and you will come to main road from Tin Hill to Bredwardine. Turn left and join it. After a while there is the luxury of narrow pavement on the left-hand side, and this borders *Brobury House*, hidden by trees and shrubs. The gardens of this Victorian mansion are open to the public at prescribed times. You now come to Bredwardine bridge, and once over it, turn left, along the *Wye Valley Walk*, into a riverside meadow. In the summer this becomes Herefordshire's answer to Bognor Regis, swimmers, paddlers, and canoeists abound. On the other side of the road, stone built *Old Court* looks down upon this scene, and has done so since the 14th century.

Bredwardine parish church lies ahead, skirt by it, first passing the entrance to the *Old Vicarage* where Kilvert lived for a short while, and continue down an avenue of trees until you join the road. Turn left into it, and you will soon be at the centre of the village and the hospitality of the *Red Lion*.

BREDWARDINE

David Verey considered Bredwardine to be 'divinely situated on the west bank of the Wye', and few would disagree. Ekwall considered that the first element in the place-name was derived from the Old English *brerd*, denoting a brim or bank, and linked to the fact that 'the place is on a slope of a steep ridge'. Shoesmith goes for *bred*, a board, rather than *brerd*, which gives us 'plank settlement': Gabby after some reflection favours Ekwall rather than Shoesmith. The second element, *worðign*, is common in Herefordshire, appearing, besides at Bredwardine, also at Leintwardine, Lugwardine, and Pedwardine. A related form appears at Hoarwithy and both forms commemorate an enclosure. Thus, 'the enclosure on the river bank' is the favoured interpretation of the place-name Bredwardine. For not very convincing reasons the name has been associated with that of *Lann Iunabui* which appears in sixth, seventh, and eighth century charters in the medieval *Liber Landavensis*. The weight of scholarship, however, identifies *Lann Iunabui* with the Herefordshire parish of *Llandinabo*.

Bredwardine in the pre-Norman times, being on the western bank of the Wye, was in the Welsh principality of Erging. Bordered by the rivers Monnow and Wye, both the Welsh form of the name Erging, and its English counterpart, Archenfield, are derived from *Ariconium*, the Roman settlement now known as Weston under Penyard, near Ross-on-Wye. Though now wholly in Herefordshire and in the diocese of Hereford, until the Norman Conquest it was thoroughly Welsh and part of the diocese of Llandaff. This is reflected in the Domesday account and the Welsh institution of *gavelkind*, whereby all a father's sons on his death shared equally in his estate and the eldest son enjoyed none of the benefits of primogeniture. This continued in Erging until its abolition by the Acts of Union of 1536 and 1542, but the Welsh language survived into the eighteenth century.

Domesday tells of the complicated social organisation existing at that time in the lordship of Bredwardine: 6 villagers, 6 smallholders, 1 man and 1 Welshman; and that they had between them 3 ploughs. There were also 3 slaves. At the Norman Conquest Bredwardine was granted to John de Bredwardine and a castle was erected as one of a chain to protect the Welsh Border, represented here by the Wye. The site of this castle is uncertain. The

OS records a motte and bailey immediately south of the parish church and Pevsner follows the RCHM in seeing this as the site of an oblong bailey, with the keep at its southern end. Further south there are traces of two fishponds. It was reconstructed by Roger Vaughan in 1639-40, as an unfortified domestic residence. It was dismantled, however, when it passed to the Cornewall family and they re-cycled the stone to build Moccas Court 1775-81, for which a local man carried out the designs of Robert Adam.

The Herefordshire antiquary, Silas Taylor, 1624-1678, wrote of 'the ancient castle of Gronw' as being at Bredwardine. This Gronw has been identified with Hywel ap Goronwy, but his murder in West Wales, related in the *Brut Tywysogion*, puts his sphere of activity far away from Herefordshire. So the identity of Silas Taylor's Gronw must remain a mystery, but the site of his castle, perhaps the one mentioned in 1227 as being held by the Baskervilles, is thought to have been a little further south of the fishponds, but still by the western bank of the Wye where the woods open out. Here excavations have revealed traces of timber and stone buildings from the 12th to the 16th centuries. Shoesmith considers that the earlier discoveries could well represent the remains of a castle or defended site, whereas the later ones belong to little more than a farmhouse complex.

The parish church, dedicated to St Andrew, belongs to at least the twelfth century, but the herringbone masonry in the north wall of the nave and the large blocked doorway in the west wall, suggest that there was an earlier, pre-Norman church which was rebuilt soon after the Conquest. This earlier church had an apse at the east end, after the fashion of Kilpeck. The Norman church has doorways in both the north and south walls of the nave. Their lintels are decorated with rosettes and the centre of that of the north door, now blocked up, has what Pevsner described as 'two strange oriental deities'. One of them has a bird's head and the other perhaps a monkey's head. There are some Norman windows in the nave and a large plain Norman font, similar in shape to those of Madley and Kilpeck. Pevsner postulates the possibility that this Norman building had a central tower, though the foundations of a tower have been identified to the north of the present Georgian structure.

Early in the 14th century a new chancel was built, somewhat askew to the nave, the reasons for this being practical rather than theological. Further changes came in fourteenth century when a handsome large three-light window was put into the rebuilt south wall of what was formerly the chancel. This new wall is also slightly askew.

On the north side of the chancel there is a mutilated late fourteenth century effigy of a knight, identified by some as Walter Baskerville, Lord of the Manor, who died in 1369. The counterbalancing sculptured alabaster effigy of another knight on the south side of the chancel is believed to be Sir Roger Vaughan, who in his day was also Lord of the Manor. He died in supporting the cause of Henry V at the Battle of Agincourt in 1415. A rood screen separated nave and chancel.

The monks of Wigmore Abbey, founded in 1179, held the advowson, ie right to appoint the vicar, until the dissolution of the monastery in 1537. Henry VIII made the appointment in 1542 and thereafter the advowson passed into private hands. The Jacobean altar table and the absence of a rood screen also represent the changes which accompanied the Reformation. The west gallery, probably introduced in 1790, when an unbuttressed tower was added to the north side of the church, was dismantled in 1875. The belfry houses six bells and the ringing chamber is on the ground floor. The oldest bell survived the demise of the previous tower, being cast in Gloucester by Abraham Rudhall II in 1729 and bears the names of Henry Davis and William Hampton, churchwardens of the day. In 1747 Abel Rudhall cast another bell, bearing the motto *Peace and Good Neighbourhood*, and John Rudhall cast two more bells for Bredwardine, in 1810 and 1826, the former being inscribed *By music minds an equal temper know*, and the latter being the heaviest in the peal, weighing seven hundred weights, two quarters, and eight pounds. Thus in the course of a hundred years the famous Rudhall foundry furnished Bredwardine parish church with four bells. They were probably floated up the Wye on rafts, and with the new tower to house them, represent a considerable expenditure at a time when the Established Church was supposed to be in a state of decline and decay. In 1928 Mears and Stainbank of Whitechapel supplied the treble and number two bell.

Bredwardine parish church was on the itinerary of the Cambrian Archaeological Association when it undertook its Herefordshire tour in August 1863. But despite the expert knowledge of the Association's members, they were baffled because though originally a small Norman church, 'it has been subsequently altered and added to in such a manner that it is not easy to make out satisfactorily the original portions'. But one conclusion they did reach which has escaped later experts. They noted that the decorated window inserted on the south wall of the nave, 'from its great similarity to some of the windows at Almeley, was probably executed by the same workmen'.

The church underwent restoration in 1875. The main external alteration was the addition of a large wooden porch of the Radnorshire style. It was inside that the changes were largely made and David Verey writing eighty years later thought the result was 'disappointing, scraped walls and ugly reredos and pews'. So much for the best endeavours of the then vicar, the Revd John Houseman, MA , and Thomas Nicholson, the Diocesan Architect, whose work became ubiquitous in Herefordshire and beyond. Neither men, however, can be held responsible for the offending reredos, installed in 1902. The roof was renewed and the gallery removed. But Verey would probably not have much regretted these developments as the introduction of what he considered 'the ugly pews'. These replaced box pews, which would nowadays be greatly treasured, but in 1875 the *Hereford Times* thought their 'ugliness and inconvenience were scarcely surpassed by any church in the county.' Wonder of wonders for the comfort loving Victorian congregation, a heating apparatus by Haden of Trowbridge was introduced and a new organ was erected in the chancel where the new choir stalls were filled with surpliced choristers according to the latest fashion. But their behaviour in the chancel was more conspicuous than in the west gallery and in October 1878 the vicar, none other than the Revd Francis Kilvert, MA, had to reprove the choristers for inattention. The encaustic tiles, probably supplied by William Godwin of Lugwardine, to replace the stone flagged floor, were not laid until 1890.

Kilvert's predecessor, the restoring Revd John Houseman, came to Bredwardine in 1871 and, died from apoplexy six years later. His sense of liturgical propriety was not always shared by his parishioners, as his successor Kilvert relates, with characteristic relish:

> I hear that Houseman at Bredwardine wishing to drape the Communion table with black on Good Friday and having no black drapery suitable for the purpose was misguided enough to put over the Table the old filthy parish pall. Everyone was disgusted and shocked at what they considered a piece of indecency. It is the talk of the country and Miss Newton is up in arms.

That was in April 1872 and Kilvert was still curate at Clyro further up the Wye valley. News travelled at a leisurely pace in those days and it took three weeks for tidings of this liturgical outrage to get into Kilvert's diary. Miss Newton, probably its source, lived at Bredwardine and a kinsman had preceded Houseman as Vicar, the Revd William Newton. The east window of the chancel was given by his widow to commemorate his death in 1862. Newton enjoyed the services of an assistant curate to help him in ministering to the pastoral needs of his 400 parishioners, or when he was away sea-bathing at Folkestone, where he died.

Kilvert was vicar here from 1877 until his death in 1879. He died prematurely aged 38 from peritonitis, a little over a month after his marriage. He is buried in the churchyard and a stone seat also commemorates him, as do the various activities of the Kilvert Society. His diary is essential for anyone interested in reading an account of rural life in the 1870s as seen by a country curate with a gift for writing charming descriptive prose.

George Jarvis, 1704-1793, also lies buried in the churchyard. Born in the parish of Staunton on Wye on the other side of the river, he spent his youth in the parish of Bredwardine before seeking his fortune in London where he was admitted as a liveryman of the Worshipful Company of Curriers in 1725. He died full of years and very wealthy in 1793 and left £30,000 in trust for the relief of the poor of Bredwardine, Staunton on Wye, and Letton. Eventually a scheme was drawn up whereby a medical officer was appointed to care for the sick in their poverty, and six poor men and six poor women maintained in almshouses to be built at Staunton. Clothing and coal clubs were established and schools in the three parishes. Suitable boys who had attended the schools, at the age of fourteen were to be apprenticed at the Trust's expense.

In 1860 a substantial complex of buildings was erected at Staunton, designed by Fulljames and Waller, the Gloucester architects. They had a busy and fashionable practice and were architects to the Dean and Chapter of Gloucester cathedral as well as to the Trustees of the Jarvis Charity. Using locally made bricks from Letton and stone facings, under a slate roof, they provided a substantial house and dispensary for the medical, a smaller house for the Clerk to the Charity, twelve almshouses, and a school which had accommodation enough to receive boarders. The buildings can still be seen on the Staunton side of the A436 to Hereford.

Kilvert relates how each Tuesday, the Jarvis Charity Trustees sent their 'charity bread and meat cart' over to Bredwardine where, in front of the *Red Lion* it would distribute allocations of bread, meat, sugar and tea to the sick, infirm, and needy of the parish. The charity was not an entirely unmixed blessing and many settled in the three parishes it served to benefit from it. Curiously named *Crafta Webb* on Bredwardine Hill was one of these squatters' settlements. It has now virtually disappeared, but in the middle of the nineteenth century could claim to have its own grocer, tailor, and shoemaker.

The Vicarage in which Kilvert lived is next to the church and in 1959 became a private house. It was built in 1805 on a grander scale than its present dimensions suggest, the servants' quarters being demolished in 1932. The vicar's stipend at Bredwardine was modest, and Kilvert took a pupil to augment it and to help in paying the wages of the housekeeper and the four other servants assisting her. But it was his sister Dora who supervised the tithe dinner in February 1878. The payment of tithes and church rates was much resented by nonconformists who saw no reason why they should support the Established Church and its clergy when they had chapels and ministers of their own to maintain. So Kilvert softened the blow with his hospitality:

> Today was the Tithe audit and tithe dinner to the farmers, both held at the Vicarage. About 50 tithe payers came, most of them very small holders, some paying as little as 9d. As soon as they had paid their tithe to Mr Heywood in the front hall they retired into the back hall and regaled themselves with bread, cheese and beer, some of them eating and drinking the value of the tithe they had paid. The tithe-paying began about 3 pm and the stream went on till six. At 7 I sat down to dinner with the farmers.

> The Pen Pistyll turkey boiled looked very noble when it came to table. At the foot of the table there was roast beef, and at the sides jugged hare and beefsteak pie, preceded by pea soup, and in due course followed by plum pudding, apple tart, mince pies and blancmange, cheese and dessert. It was a very nice dinner, thanks to Dora, and I think they all liked it and enjoyed themselves.

Until the nineteenth century travelling in Herefordshire was like hunting, there was a closed season, which could extend from October to April and it applied as much to the movement of goods as of people. The maintenance of the roads was the responsibility of the parish and Bredwardine was fortunate in having an alternative in the Wye. It was navigable as far as Glasbury in winter, though at Monnington Falls windlasses were required to help in hauling the barges. Working on the barges was dangerous and in January 1782, for example, the *Hereford Times* recorded how 'a man fell over a barge, near Bredwardine bridge and was drowned.'

In 1756 the roads in west Herefordshire were 'in divers Places so bad and ruinous, especially in the Winter Season, that Travellers and Carriages cannot pass without great Danger.' The cost of their repair was beyond the resources of the parishes through which they ran and they could neither be mended nor kept in repair, 'unless some provision be made for raising

Money to be applied for that Purpose.' The remedy was seen in setting up Turnpike Trusts, each responsible for a length of road. The trustees were local men of substance, having 'in their own right or in the right of their wives lands of the yearly value of £100 or real or personal estate worth £2000.' Each trust elected a treasurer, clerk, and surveyor and shared the profits from the tolls they charged which remained after they had repaired the roads in their care.

Setting up such a trust involved an act of Parliament and in 1757 such an act was obtained to set up the Whitney and Bredwardine Turnpike Trust with responsibility for maintaining the local section of what was to become the B4352 linking Hereford and Hay on Wye. The Trustees did well from their speculation and in one year the tolls amounted to £3,803 6s. It was time to consider building a bridge across the Wye.

The Cornewalls of Moccas maintained a ferry at Bredwardine and in 1759 another trust was established by act of Parliament to build a toll bridge across the Wye. The Cornewalls were to be compensated for their loss of revenue, and in January 1762 the Trustees contracted with Thomas Davies of Hereford to build within two years a stone six-arched bridge for a fee of £890. So as not to impede the passage of boats and barges on the river, the undersides of the arches were to be 25ft above low water level.

There was a toll house on the eastern side of the river, and the keeper collected:

> ½d per foot-passenger
> 1d per horse or other beast of burden
> 3d if the horse or other beast was drawing a cart, coach or waggon
> 5d per score for calves, sheep or swine
> 10d per score for cattle

The Trustees leased the tolls to the highest bidder and in 1878 they were then let at £35 per annum. The toll house has been gentrified into Bridge Cottage, and the bridge was repaired and reinforced in 1921 by the County Council which had acquired responsibility, on being set up in 1888, for the county's roads and bridges.

The river can rise rapidly in a matter of hours, and in February 1795 occurred 'the Greatest flood in the river Wye as was ever remembered by the Oldest Inhabitant then living In the Parish of Bredwardine'. The bridge at Bredwardine was the only one on the upper reaches of the Wye in Herefordshire to survive, and it will be recollected that the Arrow rose ten feet at Kington. Such floods were not uncommon and Kilvert records a conversation he had with a Clyro stone breaker:

> He told me how he was once travelling from Hereford to Hay by coach when the coach was wrecked in a flood by Bredwardine Bridge because the coachman would not take the bearing reins of the horses off. The bearing reins kept the horses' noses down under water, they plunged and reared and got the coach off the road and swimming like a boat, and an old lady inside screaming horribly. 'Don't keep such a noise, Ma'am,' said old Jones, throwing himself off the roof into a hedge-row against which the coach was swept by the fierce current. 'We won't leave you before we get you out somehow.' He was followed by most of the passengers on the roof, though one very tall man fell into the water on his face all along like a log, and waded through the flood out on to the Bredwardine side. One outside passenger was a miller of the neighbourhood who had a boat on the river. This was sent for and the old lady pacified and pulled into it through the coach window. The coachman was prayed and entreated to loose the bearing reins, but refused to do it. Two horses were drowned, one wheeler went down under the pole. The other, a leader, broke loose and plunged and pawed and reared at the bridge out of the flood till he was exhausted, and then fell over backwards into the stream and was rolled away by the current.

In Kilvert's time at Bredwardine there occurred in November 1878 what he believed to be the second greatest flood of the century:

> The previous night the river had risen so high that it almost covered the road by the toll cottage. The next evening the floodwaters rose even more and his Churchwarden, Mr T Stokes of Old Court, rode down to the bridge on his horse to see if help was needed. By then the water was up to the girths of his horse.

A month later flooding gave way to freezing, and children were sliding, at their peril, on the half frozen river below Bredwardine bridge. At Moccas things were safer and the river was entirely frozen over. Such was degree of freezing that by end of the year parishioners at Bredwardine found themselves on all fours or crawling on their hands and knees along their frozen lanes. Then came the thaw and all was recorded by Kilvert:

> Sudden thaw and break up of the frozen river. Huge masses and floes of ice have been coming down the river all day, rearing,

crushing, grinding against each other, and thundering against the bridge. A crowd of people were on the bridge and watching the ice pass through the arches.

A far speedier and more comfortable alternative to the stage coach or the carrier's waggon travelling along the turnpike became available in 1864 when the Midland Railway opened its line from Hereford to Hay-on-Wye. Kinnersley, four miles away, was the nearest station to Bredwardine and had four trains in each direction on weekdays, taking 29 minutes to get to Hereford and 15 minutes to Hay. In December 1918, when post war euphoria was at its height, Bredwardine planned to make the land locally more fit for heroes by connecting the village directly to Hereford by light railway. There was considerable enthusiasm for the project but no financial support and it came to nothing. The mainline railway survived until December 1962.

In 1852 Bredwardine, besides the usual crop of farmers, had a blacksmith, a wheelwright, a tailor, two shoe makers, and a clock and watch maker. Most of them, no doubt, refreshed themselves at the *Red Lion* or its rival, which has long since disappeared, the *Three Horse Shoes*, down by the bridge.

Pevsner approved of the architecture of the *Red Lion*, describing it as a 'very nice late C17 brick house with hipped roof'. Consisting of five two-storey bays, their leaded wooden framed windows have their original form, undisfigured by double glazing, with their wooden mullions and transoms. A pedimented gable surmounts this frontage and contributes to its overall dignity. Standing physically at the centre of the village, it was also at the centre of its social life. In the nineteenth century the magistrates met here to administer justice, as did the churchwardens to settle the affairs of the parish.

———————

Red Lion, Bredwardine

Walk 5: Bredwardine to Arthur's Stone and back

Starting from Bredwardine, walk up the lane on the right hand side of the *Red Lion*, there is a little cluster of modern houses on the left, with a stream, and trees. It was a very still, atmospheric, late autumnal day when we did this walk, and the trees were still holding on to their last vestiges of colour. Pass *Cockpits* on the right; house names such as these raise the question: are they historical? Was it here in the eighteenth century that the parishioners of Bredwardine indulged their appetite for cruelty and gambling with a little furtive cockfighting? Throwing stones at cocks was a traditional pastime of apprentices on Shrove Tuesday, but in the early nineteenth century this kind of leisure activity was steadily suppressed.

At *Springfield* on the left Kilvert fans may care to make a very short diversion, following the direction of the finger board, down the lane, passing on the right a lane-like entrance to another house. Pass on the left the *Croft*, another popular house name derived from the Old English for an enclosed field. In the process of time the word came to denote a small plot of arable land adjacent to a house, eventually becoming the polite, Betjemanesque name for a select building site.

Then comes Bredwardine school where Kilvert taught the children their Prayer Book catechism. This reinforced the social *status quo* by emphasising their duties to God and man, and the importance of knowing their place in society:

> My duty towards my Neighbour, is to love him as myself, and to do to all men, as I would they should do unto me: To love, honour, and succour my father and mother: To honour and obey the queen, and all that are put in authority under her: To submit myself to all my governors, teachers, spiritual pastors and masters: To order myself lowly and reverently to all my betters: To hurt no body by word nor deed: To be true and just in all my dealing: To bear no malice nor hatred in my heart: To keep my hands from picking and stealing, and my tongue from evil-speaking, lying, and slandering: To keep my body in temperance, soberness, and chastity: Not to covet nor desire other men's goods; but to

learn and labour truly to get mine own living, and to do my duty in that state of life, unto which it shall please God to call me.

In 1822 Sir George Cornewall, Bart, the local grandee and lord of the manor, from Moccas Court built a school at Bredwardine, on behalf of the Trustees of the Jarvis Charity. That was replaced by the present building which shows every sign of being the work of Fulljames and Waller, the Gloucester architects. In 1860 they built the much larger set of school buildings for the Jarvis Charity at Staunton-on-Wye. The Bredwardine building provided a school room, store room for the clothing supplied by the Trust for the three parishes, and a house for the Schoolmaster. The attendance of some pupils was erratic, and hop-picking, the delights of the Eardisley fair,

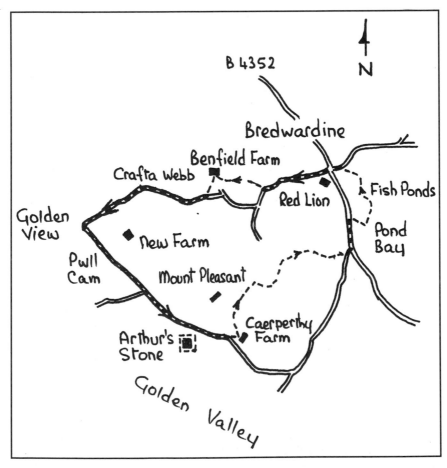

and the excitement of following the hunt all contributed to the pupils' truancy. The school closed in 1969 and is now a private house.

Now retrace your steps to the lane, and continue your ascent of Bredwardine Hill which attains a height of 291 metres. At this stage the going is quite tough, being 1 in 5. This is part of the *Wye Valley Trail*, and finger boards point the direction, both up and down the hill. Pass *Cwm Farm* on the left. Names on this side of the Wye are often in Welsh, for we are now in the heart of *Herefordia in Wallia*. The Welsh *Cwm* and its English form *Combe*, as in *Ilfracombe*, denotes a valley and is in both cases evidence for what was once a Welsh speaking population.

Mercifully the gradient now eases. By a turning to the right there is stile. Cross it and thereby leave the *Wye Valley Trail*. Head now for the tree, which is slightly to the right, and by it, to the left, there is a stile. Cross it, and follow the arrow straight ahead. *Benfield Farm* is beyond the next field, and looking behind, one is rewarded by fantastic views over Herefordshire beyond the Wye. Following the arrows, make for the iron gate on the other side of the field. Another arrow takes one ahead, and through the gate, bearing right, enter the yard of *Benfield Farm*.

This takes you past, to the right, two barns, one ancient and one modern. Then join a lane, and bear left up it. You will soon come to a gate on the right hand side, with an arrow and a request to keep the dog on the lead. This is a bridle path. There is a modern cottage type homestead on the left, and the countryside is now becoming rather more wooded. Follow the base of the hill round to the right until you approach an iron gate on your left. Go through the gate with its sign as a bridle way, and you come on to a lane, with which you made an earlier acquaintance when you first left Bredwardine. Turn right into the lane, pass some stone built cottages on the left. Trees on either side make it pleasant walking and there is very little traffic. Ignore the bridle path to the left, pass *Holy Bush Cottage*, also on the left, the entrance to *Lane Cottage* on the right, and *Glebe Cottage*. If this latter name is of any antiquity it commemorates the glebe land of the local incumbent. It was part of his benefice and he farmed it, or, if he was disinclined so to do, rented it out.

The Ordnance survey map names this area as *Crafta Webb*, and it is something of a lost village. There was here in the middle of the 19th century a collection of unpretentious cottages, each hastily thrown together so that their occupants could claim, by virtue of their residence in the parish, the benefits of the Jarvis Charity. The settlement had its own grocer, tailor and shoemaker, and the size of its population is indicated by the numbers attending

Kilvert's cottage lectures during the winter. As many as thirty-five would crowd into one of these cottages, long since disappeared, for a lecture on some religious subject or other. It wasn't that those who lived at *Crafta Webb* were particularly devout, but rather their attendance would enhance their claims upon the Charity, and there was little other entertainment on offer besides that offered, for better or worse, by the Vicar who also happened to be a trustee of the charity.

The lane now wends its upward way to the left, past the stone built *Lower Barn* and *Old Castle*, now restored and gentrified, and *New Farm*, through the field, on the left. The lane bears to the left, past a footpath sign on the right to *Golden View*. Continue on, past *Pwll Cam*, the Crooked Pool. *Gam* [the soft mutation of 'c' in Welsh is 'g'] is quite a common surname, originally denoting someone who was lame. David Gam, despite his disability, shone at Agincourt, and *Heol Gam* appears in Welsh towns as the name of a winding street.

The lane now follows a remarkably straight course, almost Roman in character. We are reminded that in earlier times hill top travel was much easier than travelling along marshy, densely wooded valley floors. Below us to the right is the mis-named *Golden Valley*. The Welsh form is *Ystrad Dwr*, dwr meaning water, which the Normans saw as *d'or*, or golden. The *dwr* of *Ystrad Dwr* is linguistically linked with the place-name *Dover* in Kent, the connection of which with water is self-evident, and is a reminder of a time when the British predecessor of modern Welsh was heard as much at Dover and Edinburgh as at Llandaff.

Continue down the lane, passing a turning to the right warning the motorist of the 1 in 5 descent ahead of them into the Golden Valley. Then after a slight bend to the left, Arthur's Stone awaits you on the right.

Well displayed information tells us that we are standing at the threshold of a late neolithic chamber dating between 3700 BC and 2700 BC. These massive stones formed a burial vault with an entrance tunnel set under a large mound of earth now destroyed. The tomb was probably used for the burial of members of a family or community for several hundred years.

Those stalwart members of the Cambrian Archaeological Association so often referred to on our present travels attempted to visit this site in August 1863, but failed to make it. Access was then by an unmade track that defeated the strength of their horses and the springs of their carriages. But one of their more energetic members, the noted Victorian archaeologist, EL Barnwell, *did* visit the site a few years later. He rightly doubted whether it had any connection with King Arthur, who supposedly led the resistance to Anglo-Saxon invasions in the early decades of the 6th century AD. The distribution of Arthurian legends throughout Dark Age Britain makes it more than likely that Arthur was a composite semi-historical figure of many manifestations. Wrote Barnwell:

> As usual it is associated with King Arthur, it being called by the peasants *Arthur's Stone*; they, however, probably apply the term only to the large covering slab and not the whole structure. No careful collection of such instances of Arthur's name has yet been made, but probably all the more important masses of stone throughout Wales will be found so associated.

The site is now in the care of English Heritage and no mention is made of King Arthur.

But back to the walk, continue along the lane, past the drive on the left to *Mount Pleasant*, a touch of Bath and the 18th century in upland Herefordshire. A few yards further on a finger board directs you over a stile on the left, just before *Caeperthy Farm*. Another Welsh name. *Cae* denotes a field, and *perth* a bush or hedge, and *ty* a house. So perhaps this is a com-

Arthurs' Stone, Bredwardine

memoration to 'the house by the hedged field' made by the Welsh speaking ancestors of its present occupants.

Once over the stile, with a gate by it, follow the hedge to your right and continue across the field. Over the stile, following the direction of the arrow, one arrives at two gates, side by side. Take the left one, indicated by the arrow. Continue along the margin of the field. The hedge is still on the right and there are glimpses of spectacular views through hedge. There are two arrows at the next stile, one points to the left and the other straight on. Carry straight on. More fine views are visible here, this time towards Ladylift, beyond the Wye Valley.

Ahead are the ruins of a stone farmhouse and its boundary walls. Walk to the right of these ruins down hill to a stile. Once over the stile, bear immediately left, following the guidance of the arrow. The path now drops quite sharply and the going is a little rough. With trees to your left, drop down further to a little dingle. Arriving at a stile and gate, the arrow will direct you, but first admire yet another splendid view ahead. The descent continues. When we walked these paths, the quiet was broken by a power glider above us. What views he had of a well wooded landscape, interspersed with fields and hedges, and farmsteads! There is a dingle to the left, and a stile ahead. Following the arrow, continue down the hill, with a hedge now to the left. Through the gate to the left at the bottom, bear left, following the margin of the field for a little while until you arrive at a gate. Looking ahead down the hill you can see Bredwardine church and its white washed vicarage. Our path stills drops sharply, the hedge is now to the right.

There is now a choice of paths: take the bridle path through the gate, bear to the right and follow the hedge on the right to the corner of the field. We now descend into another dingle and continuing through it we arrived at a gate, rather than a stile, it still being a bridle path. A little way on, another gate gives access to an open field. Turn left and on arriving at the bottom of the field there is another gate which gives access to a lane. Turn left into it, and in a little while there is a road. To the right this road ascends Dorstone Hill on its way to the village of Dorstone in the Golden Valley. But we turn left and soon turn left again into the B4352 from Hereford to Bredwardine and Hay on Wye. There is no footpath, and for a short while the way is rather perilous, and the usual precautions should be applied.

Leave the B4352 at the appearance on the right hand side of the road, of a gate way and a footpath sign. Turn into the field and follow the hedge on the left until you come to a sign directing you across a stile. There are two arrows, and once over, bear left and cross a small wooden bridge, with another stile at the end. We are at Pond Bay, the pond being to the right, separating you from the Wye beyond. Continue on through a pleasant glade, with glimpses of the lake to your right, and its swans. This is a bridle path, with gates rather than stiles, so go through the next gate and follow the direction ahead. We are now near the site of Bredwardine castle.

Veer for a short way to the right, and then to the left, those with an archaeological interest may wish to pause to look for evidence of the medieval fishponds and what little is left of earthworks of the motte and bailey of the castle itself. One has now arrived at Bredwardine churchyard which the bridle path skirts to the left. On arriving at an avenue of trees, turn left into it. This takes you to the road linking Bredwardine to the A438. Turn left into towards Bredwardine and in a short distance you will arrive at the village centre and the *Red Lion.*

BOLLINGHAM

Domesday speaks of Bollingham as *Burardestune*, which evolved by way of *Bolynghull* and *Bollinghill* to the modern Bollingham, a form known by 1608. Dr Margaret Gelling, the Ekwall of our day, has suggested that Domesday's *Burardestune* evolved from the Old English *burhweard*, meaning 'guardian of the fort'. In so doing she places Bollingham, and similar place-names in Herefordshire and neighbouring Shropshire, in a Mercian system of defensive posts, which antedate Offa's 8th century dyke. If this be so, then the mighty Offa, who had dealings with Charlemagne himself, had to concede land to the Welsh, for Bollingham lies west of the course of the dyke.

When the Cambrians set out from Kington on the 28th August 1863 on their long day of sightseeing, the first building they visited was the medieval chapel of Bollingham. Its status became that of a chapel of ease for the convenience of the parishioners of Eardisley living hereabouts at the remotest extreme from their parish church. But its original role must have been to serve the small motte and bailey castle, which in Norman times replaced its Mercian fortlet predecessor. It intrigued the Cambrians:

> Close to the church is a small tumulus, which from its size might be sepulchral, but is more probably, from its situation, the remains of a small castle. It is now surmounted with a building, the upper part of which is used as a pigeon-house, the lower as a domestic office, being probably an unique instance of such use of an ancient earthwork.

In 1863, of course, there was no Royal Commission on the Historical Monuments of England, [known, rather less grandly, since 1999 as English Heritage], to protect and advise on the monuments of our national heritage. The Bollingham earthwork is on private property and is not accessible to the public.

Bollingham chapel, with its unusual dedication to St Silas, the companion and fellow worker of St Paul, enjoys a singularly attractive site. Surrounded by trees and well kept grass, there is a retiring modesty about the building. It consists of a simple nave and chancel, with a bellcote for two bells, though only one was employed, and under a moss covered roof of stone tiles. When the Cambrians saw it in 1863 it had yet to be restored.

The excursionists started at an earlier hour this morning on account of the length of the day's work, which commenced with a visit to Bollingham Chapel, a primitive building of the thirteenth century, if not older. The whole structure is of the rudest character, without the slightest ornament or moulding. A large, broad buttress without offsets, surmounted with a plain gable overtopping the roof of the church, occupies the greater part of the external east end, through which is pierced a small narrow deeply splayed single light, and which is probably one of the smallest east windows in existence. One or two more similar early windows are on the north side, the principal light being afforded by a large square modern opening above the pulpit.

Four years later the chapel was restored by Thomas Nicholson the diocesan architect at a cost of £583. The nave and chancel were given new roofs, though their fine 14th or 15th century timber beams survived, and the west and north walls were rebuilt and a south porch added. The windows were re-glazed, the floors paved, and pitch pine pews installed. Godwin tiles were laid in the chancel. The stained glass in the east window is by the prestigious firm of Clayton and Bell, it illustrates the *Te deum*, with the Lamb of God in the topmost medallion. It was given by his widow in memory of the Revd William St Leger Aldworth, MA, an Irishman from County Cork, and incumbent of Eardisley 1862-66.

The glass in the west window is by Heaton, Butler & Bayne, who exhibited at the Great Exhibition of 1851. In two lancets of coloured patterned glass the scriptural text in one widow reminds the viewer, quoting the first verse of Psalm 41, that 'Blessed is he that considereth the poor: the Lord will deliver him in the time of trouble.' The text in the other widow, 'Here we have no continuing city, but we seek one to come' is a quotation from the *Epistle to the Hebrews*, 13:14.

The windows were the gift of the Dowager Lady Cockburn in memory of Richard Whitcombe, late of Bollingham, 1761-1829, his wife Sarah, 1770-1847, and 'their talented son' Richard Whitcombe, Barrister at Law, 1794-1854. The Whitcombes haled from Kington where Richard Whitcombe, junior was baptized. His sister, Anne Whitcombe, married the Revd Francis Coke of Lemore, 1788-1856, and in 1834 Anne, their eldest daughter, married Sir William Sarsfield Rossiter Cockburn, 1796-1858, of Downton House, near New Radnor, and of port wine fame.

Francis Coke of Lemore, whose father Richard Coke was inducted as vicar of Eardisley in 1753, was an accomplished pluralist. The wedding of his daughter Anne and William Cockburn took place at Gladestry where he had been absentee rector since 1810. He was also vicar of Sellack in Herefordshire, and a prebendary of Hereford cathedral. Thus, it was Anne Coke, the widow of Sir William Cockburn, who gave the west window of Bollingham chapel in memory of her brother and parents. Bollingham's connection with the Cokes of Lemore is also commemorated by its 17th century chalice, fitted with a paten which can also serve as its lid. It bears the arms of Dr George Coke, bishop of Hereford, who retired to nearby Lemore Manor during the Commonwealth.

There was another restoration in 1890 and Pevsner denounced its 'horrid stone font and pulpit.' In the chancel there is a 'Cusson's Patent Positive Organ', though it is some time since its pipes have made music, its duties having been taken over by an electronic successor. The gas lights have also been electrified. A memorial on the north wall of the nave records, once again, the great debt these country churches owe their churchwardens. It remembers with gratitude Cecil Williams who died in 1992 'after serving here as churchwarden for over forty years'.

The office of churchwarden is both ancient and honourable. The canons of 1604 prescribe that churchwardens are to be chosen by the incumbent and the parishioners, and if they fail to agree, then one is to be appointed by the incumbent, and the other by the people. The election takes place annually at the Easter vestry, and the wardens are responsible for the material condition of the parish church and, in days gone by, for the orderly behaviour of the parishioners in an around the church. They attend, to give an account of their stewardship, the archdeacon's annual visitation which, is suspended every third year for that of the bishop.

In 1582 the churchwardens complained at the bishop's visitation, that the chapel yard needed fencing. The parishioners were to put the matter in hand by midsummer or else be fined 5s. In 1625 there were more complaints about the fencing, and about the condition of the windows, vestments, and the cushion on the altar for the missal. All were in disrepair.

The churchyard not only offered pasture for the incumbent's sheep, but also served as an unofficial playground, and in this the parishioners of Bollingham were no exception. In 1598:

> William Kedward *alias* Rowlands was excommunicated for playing at tennis at the time of divine service in the chapel yard.

In 1608 there was a more serious matter for consideration, again involving the Kedwards:

Joan Kedward of the chapel of Bollingham is noted for incontinence with Walter Powell, servant of Humphrey East of Queest Moor [just north of Lemore], gent.

Summoned to the ecclesiastical court, as she was, Joan Kedward did not appear, thereby committing contempt of court.

The churchwardens also ensured that the parish clerk kept the registers properly. In 1710 the registers recorded that a certain Roger was baptised at Bollingham, an event neither he nor his parents Evan and Damaris Davis of Crickadarn in Breconshire could have expected, for he was 'in itinere natus', born on the journey. Churchwardens were not paid for their services, though they could claim their expenses and 'for ale for their trouble.'

Not everyone who lived at Bollingham felt that the Reformation in general and the Church of England in particular were good things. Amongst these was a certain Mr Somerset, a kinsman of the Earl of Worcester, and who shared the family's Roman Catholicism. Indeed, disregarding the provisions of the Act of Uniformity of 1662 which required all to worship according to the Anglican Book of Common Prayer, he engaged the services of Charles Kerne, a Roman Catholic priest from Weobley, to say mass for him at Bollingham.

The matter was brought to the attention of the authorities and on 4th August 1679 Kerne stood trial 'for being a Romish priest' at Hereford Assizes before Lord Chief Justice Scroggs. Remembered as 'an intemperate man, with a brazen face, coarse manners, a loud voice, and a brutal tongue', neither Scroggs's private nor his public character would apparently bear much examination. It is a credit, therefore, to the English jury system that Kerne was acquitted.

Where did Mr Somerset live? It was more probably at *Bollingham Farm*, than at *Bollingham House*. Bollingham House, despite its Victorian appearance, is rather like an architectural onion. There is a Victorian skin, given to the house by Richard Drew, the London architect who designed Hergest Croft in 1896, rebuilt Lady Hawkins Grammar School, and restored Kington parish church in 1873/4. Beneath this is a Georgian house and under that, there is a timber framed medieval predecessor. In 1679 the house was in the ownership of William Badham, whose family had owned it since 1610 and did so until 1760. No Mr Somersets are mentioned during this period.

Walk 6: Almeley to Kington with the Bollingham option

Leave the *Bells,* and turn right up the hill, past the *Old Vicarage* on the left, cross over the road and turn left into *Manor Close.* Pass the *Old Coach House* on the left, and enter into *Ashcroft*, continuing until there is ahead of you a stile with a dog bar. The finger post is three directional, chose the option allowing you to continue straight ahead. Cross the field to a stile by a gate, following the sign, you will soon see a finger post offering four options. Choose the one that takes you straight on ahead. Keep to the right of the fence when you meet it, though the direction given by the finger post was a little ambiguous, suggesting you should go left of the fence. If in doubt in these situations, always let the map be the final arbiter. *Hawthorn Farm* is to the right on the other side of the field. Look back, and if it is a fine day, there will be a spectacular view of the *Black Mountains*, and if you are lucky, even the *Brecon Beacons* beyond.

Over the stile, follow the arrow, the hedge will now be on your right. We are walking now under a row of oak trees which once served as a boundary, but the fence has been removed. The footpath now drops down steeply for a short descent. At the bottom some steps give access to a stile and a footbridge over the stream. This played an important role in the earlier life of Almeley, supplying it with water for daily life, feeding the Old Castle moat, and providing power for the mill. A trackway awaits us, and so once over the bridge, turn right.

We are now walking along the route of the old 1820 Kington Tramway. One can imagine meeting a pair of horses, in tandem, laboriously hauling a train of two or three trams through the dingle, bringing lime from the Old Radnor limekilns, not only for the local farms, but also for those in south Wales. Passing in the opposite direction, the trams would be full of coal and manufactured goods from south Wales. Pass *FirTree Cottage* on the left and arriving at a three directional finger post, take the rather more narrow public footpath going off uphill to the left.

At the top an arrow directs one's path ahead over the dog friendly stile. Soon after turn left at the next stile and you will see *Wootton Farm* ahead of you. Continue across the field to the corner where a stile with a dog board takes you onto the lane from Almeley. Bear left, and after some farm buildings the lane divides. Then take the left branch, a public footpath sign directing your way. The new path soon bears to the right, and where this starts, go through a gate on the left hand side, and leave the lane. An arrow directs your way to a path through the field, taking you down hill. Go through the next gate and follow the direction of the arrow, with the hedge more or less on your right,

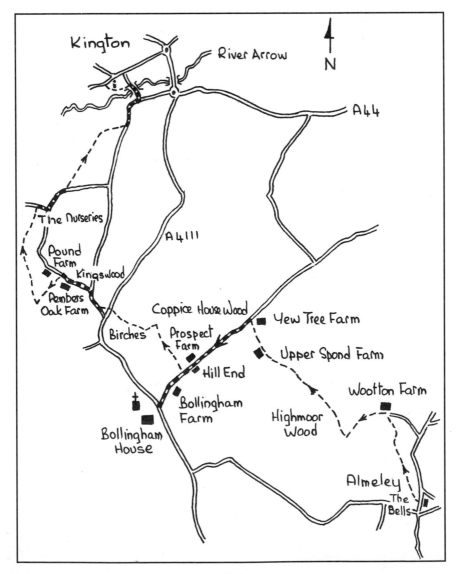

enjoying more fine views of the *Black Mountains* and the *Brecon Beacons* beyond.

Go through the gate at the end of the field, following the direction of the arrow and continue with the hedge on the right. Pass a gate on the right, and make for the gate in the hedge facing you ahead on the far side of the field. Through the gate, a finger board gives the direction, turning right on to a farm track which takes us past some water troughs, and then *Highmoor Wood* on the left. Keep on now, with the wood always to the left. Through the gate ahead of us, and vere slightly to the left across the field.

The field now narrows, and go over the stile ahead into the next field. This stile has both a dog board and an arrow to direct us. *Highmoor Wood* is still to the left and a hedge to the right. Make for the gate in the top right hand corner of the field, and follow the arrow. The stile beside the gate was badly damaged when we did this walk. Still keeping to the right, make for the stile, which is ahead in the top right hand corner of the field. *Upper Spond Farm* can now be seen a few fields ahead.

Go through the gate and across the next field. We are now beyond *Highmoor Wood* on the left, and are still following the hedge to our right. The *Black Mountains* can now be seen, weather permitting, on your left. Go through the gate at the top right hand corner of the field, and on to a farm track, which will take us through *Upper Spond Farm*, the older, 16th century buildings being on the left. The meaning of the name *Spond* is something of a mystery, but the Derbyshire place-name *Spondon* has been identified as denoting 'the hill where shingles were made'. This is assuming, of course, that our *Spond* is derived from the Old English *spon*. In such a wooded area as this, however, it is not unlikely that wooden shingles were used for roofing. A stone slab on the floor of the nave of Bollingham chapel records the death of Sarah Harper, *née* Higgins, of '*Spon*', who died in 1711. The burial of her relation, Ann Higgins of Bollingham, is recorded for 1650.

Carry on down the lane past the farm. The lane is high-sided with holly, hazel nuts and blackberries in its hedges. Pass the finger board on your left and another farm to the right. This is a stylish brick and stone L-shaped farm house, of the late 18th and early 19th centuries, and retains some of its original windows.

There is a T-junction ahead and the road to left runs to Bollingham, and to the right to Lyonshall. Turn left here for Bollingham, pass *Yew Tree Farm* on the right, and walk for two thirds of a mile until you pass *Prospect Farm* on the right and *Hill End* on the left. Continue on for a short distance until a finger post on the right directs you to a foot path, through an iron gate.

It is here that those interested in architecture make a diversion to Bollingham church, about a third of a mile further on down the road. At the end of the road you pass *Bollingham Farm*, with its 17th century farm house, on the left. Cross the main Kington-Hereford road, the A4111, with some care, and Bollingham chapel is immediately above the conifer-protected *Bollingham House*.

Leaving Bollingham to rejoin the walk, cross the A4111 and retrace your path up the Lyonshall lane opposite until after a third of a mile you see again the finger post on the left-hand side of the lane, pointing your way through the iron gate, putting you back on line.

Follow the hedge on your left, passing an agricultural roller, and continue to the iron gate at the top of the field. Continue with the hedge still on your left and the fine views of the Black Mountains beyond. Through another iron gate at the top of the field, with a yellow arrow pointing our direction ahead, follow the hedge on the left, with *Coppice House Wood* on the right.

At the top of the field a finger post offers the alternatives of turning either to the left or to the right. Take the left-hand option and cross a stile. The hedge is now on your right and to the left, weather permitting, are panoramic views of Herefordshire. Arriving at a rather lofty stile on the right, follow the arrow and cross it. Then cross a grassy lane and go over the stile confronting you. A yellow arrow directs your path across the meadow, and go through the gate on the other side, and following the arrow, cross this field with the hedge and trees on your left. Even though it was late autumn when we did this walk there were still a few buttercups in flower.

Go through the gate at the top of the field, there is a fence of wire netting and trees on the left, and follow along its course. You will see *The Birches* to the left. Now bear right and then left passing a pond. Go through a wooden gate on the right and continue ahead as the arrow directs. Following the hedge on your left, there is another small pond on your right, and you will soon arrive at a sign posted stile, complete with dog gate giving access to the busy A4111 Kington-Hereford road.

Cross the road with care and go up the lane, slightly to your left on the other side, sign posted for Kingswood and the Small Breeds Farm. Pass *Juniper Cottage* on the right and then *Bank Villa*, also on the right, with white iron railings and gates which look as if they came from Meredith's foundry in Kington.

The Merediths of Kington were ironmongers in the 18th century. In 1819 John Meredith, 1758-1823, invested £300 in the new Kington Tramway. A fellow investor was James Watt, no doubt well able to point out that the tramway would contribute to the prosperity of his expanding business by supplying it competitively with iron and coal. Another factor contributing to Meredith's prosperity was that he supplied the rails. About the year 1820 Meredith purchased a site at *Sunset*, at the end of Victoria Road and just before the roundabout, from Lord Oxford and erected a foundry and its accompanying workshops. Its dignified gateway still survives, as does the bell in the bellcote above which announced the start and finish of the working day at 6 am and 6pm. The power was provided by a water wheel through which the bellows, hammers, and other machinery were operated. Nails long remained a principal product and a complex of ten cottages, known as *Nailers' Row*, and eight forges was built nearby. It became almost a matter of honour for local citizens to be buried, not in wool, as was once the case, but in nails. Thus, when a well known doctor died in 1808 his coffin was provided by John Meredith of Kington, lined with ten yards of superfine crepe held in place by 500 locally made tin tacks. In 1882 135 men and boys worked at the Foundry and in *Nailers' Row*. It closed in 1901 and since then its buildings have had a career as a laundry and now comprise a complex of craft workshops. But many local farms and houses still have old gates, railings, and fences, from Meredith's foundry.

Returning to the walk, beyond *Bank Villa*, pass a brick and stone-built cottage on the left-hand side, with a footpath sign nearby directing a way off to the left. Ignore this and continue along the lane. Then turn left into another lane at a junction by the *Rowans*, a stone built cottage, with a letter box on the wall. Pass the old style red telephone kiosk on the left and *Pool House* on the right. The lane winds its way and you will pass *Pember's Oak Farm*, originally timber framed, but re-fronted in brick and stone, on the left. In the seventeenth century Francis Pember was one of the local worthies who contributed towards what was then the extremely well furnished library of the newly founded Lady Hawkins' Free School in Kington.

We are now in *Kingswood*. The wood has long since disappeared and the king from whom it derived its name, like nearby Kington, was Harold, c.1020-1066. Some of the hedges bordering the lane are cropped and pleached in the traditional fashion. The method of cropping and pleaching varies in different counties, but the finished result is not only an example of surviving agricultural craftsmanship, but a far more efficient hedge, offering much better winter protection to the stock it encloses, than one shaped by a hedge cutter. Hedging competitions are still a feature of the rural calendar, especially in upland areas.

Pass *Green Gables* on the right and arriving at a signpost on the left, cross the style, newly installed, like the wooden gate beside it, and go down a tree-lined lane. Pass *Pound Farm*, being restored, on your right. Now stone faced, this was originally timber framed and some of its 14th and 15th century timber roof-work survives. Fashion as well as the hazard of fire caused many timber framed houses to acquire less flammable exterior walls. The name carried by the house, *The Pound*, is probably as old as the building itself. Originally it would have commemorated the enclosure established up by the Lord of the Manor for the detention of stray and trespassing cattle of his tenants. Until they were redeemed their owners had the right of access to feed them.

Having passed the farm house, bear right, as the arrow directs, and continue, with the trees to your left, making for the stile ahead. Once over the stile, don't follow the arrow, but turn to your right and follow the hedge, also on your right. The path now descends, cross the stile on your right, and follow the arrow diagonally left across the field. The terrain becomes overgrown at the bottom of the field, and without carefully following the map, finding the stile amongst it could be difficult. However, amongst the under growth there *is* a stile, and its arrow points the way ahead.

Continue through the scrub, with a ditch on your left, still travelling down hill. The OS map gives this area the name *The Golden Pippin*. Originally a *pippin*, as with its relative a *pip*, referred to the seed of any fleshy fruit, but in the process of time it came to refer specifically to an apple tree grown from seed, as opposed to being grafted on to a stock. Such varieties as *Golden Pippin, Ribston Pippin, Blenheim Pippin*, and of course, in more recent times, *Cox's Orange Pippin*, have all enjoyed popularity in the orchard. Herefordshire is well known for its orchards, and both fruit trees and hops were still grown locally in the early nineteenth century. James Watt sent his Kington friends various varieties of apple and pear trees from his Handsworth estate near Birmingham. Herefordshire cider, of course, has long been famous and in 1720 the Duke of Chandos sent his Genoan picture dealer 'forty dozen Herefordshire Redstreak Cider'. HP Bulmer, whose father, the Revd Charles Henry Bulmer, MA, the rector of Credenhill, had a great interest in growing fruit trees, founded his cider business in Hereford in 1887. It was at a similar date that two Victorian ladies, Miss Ellis and Miss Bull, produced, in two folio volumes, *The Herefordshire Pomona*. 'Drawn and coloured from nature' and with 'descriptions of the most esteemed kinds of apples and pears', it is a monument of Victorian art and scholarship. Returning to our directions for the walk, continue on down hill, an arrow, pointing ahead on a gate post will reassure you that all is well [though the fence adjoining the post has gone]. Continue through the scrub, you eventually arrive at a stile, cross it and the ditch beyond it by a wide plank. The going is now much easier, follow the fence to your right, the ground is now rising, and there are views of Radnorshire to your left, their austerity contrasting with those of Herefordshire.

Cross the next stile and follow the arrow across the field. There is a stone and colour-washed cottage to your right. Make for the right-hand corner of the field where there is a stile and a broken finger post by it. Had it still been in repair it would have shown, as the OS map does, that this is the isolated meeting place of five public footpaths. Take the path that descends the undulating field to a stile with the hedge to the right. Cross the stile and, following the arrow, aim for the electricity pole. The going is now uphill and *The Nurseries*, hidden by trees, but marked on the map, are in front of you.

Cross the stile, which has a dog gate, at last, and follow the arrow ahead, with a hedge to your right. Through the iron gate ahead, with a finger board to its left, and this gives access to a lane. Turn right into the lane, pass *Bramble Cottage* on your right and *Quarry House* on your left. Then, arriving at a lane on your left, turn into it.

Pass the TV and radio mast on the left and there is a sign-posted stile just beyond, also to your left. Once over the stile, *Bradnor Hill* can be seen ahead on the other side of Kington, but bear diagonally to the right across this field making for the stile in the hedge beyond. Passing to the left of the solitary silver birch in the field one arrives at the stile, having noticed the blades of a water pump in the trees ahead, and passing under electricity wires which have transformed rural life.

Having arrived at the stile, don't be distracted by the adjacent cattle grid leading on to *Old Ashmore House*, attractive and brick built, instead, negotiate the stile which is rather insecure, and follow the path through a little copse. Do not be alarmed by a pack of little dogs barking with all their might behind the fence to your right, for you will soon arrive at another stile, with an oak to its left. Climb over and follow the footpath diagonally across the field, aiming for two isolated trees in the cropped and pleached hedge. Make for the stile between them and climb over. With the sound of barking still ringing in our ears, we were grateful for Gabby's unwillingness to participate. Barking is not a characteristic of the greyhound, and their owners' households are usually all the better for it.

Once over the stile, walk diagonally to the right until you meet the tree-lined margin of the field which surmounts a very deep drainage ditch. The hills of north Herefordshire now provide your view, and continue to make for a sign posted gate to the right, and contemplate the view ahead of Kington. It displays the town as a compact unity, whilst at the same time showing the various developments which took place in its nine hundred years of history. The parish church on the hill overlooks its urban charge; the neat classical profile of *Ridgebourne* set in its park land, and the old Grammar School are below it. The primary school and the recreation ground are further below, and the four-square Methodist Chapel still stands out proudly though long abandoned as a place of worship. The handsome terrace of three early Victorian status town houses looks down upon the rest of the town from the *Square*. And behind it all is the back-cloth of *Bradnor Hill,* surmounted by its golf course.

But to return to our route: now through the gate one continues on straight ahead for a while before turning gradually to the left, dropping down steadily, to a gate at the furthermost corner of the field, whilst to the left there is another interesting view of Kington. The gate, at which we have now arrived, opens upon Kingswood Road. Now turn left, and rest if you want on the thoughtfully placed wooden seat, before walking down into the town, noticing the toll house at the bottom of the road as you turn left into the main road leading into Kington. Across the *Arrow*, one turns immediately left, and then right at the mill ahead of you, and just before the yard of *Turner's Mill.* Admire the miller's stone-built house and its lunetted pediment and enjoying the buildings of the yard as you pass by, to arrive by way of a sign-posted footpath, in the *Mill Street* car park. This is just above the *Market Hall* and the *Information Centre* where the walk to Almeley began.

LETTON

Ekwall considered that the place-name Letton, was in origin 'no doubt *Leac-tun*, as in Leighton, the tun where leeks are grown'. Domesday tells of Tesselin who held the manor from Roger de Lacy, and leased it to Edwy Young who 'could go where he would'. Mention is made, too, of the fact that 'a priest and 7 settlers with 1 plough pay 5s'. There was also 'a mill that pays nothing and 2 slaves'. The seven colonists were invited to settle by the lord on his land to cultivate it. They would have been useful in bringing new and waste-lands under the plough in this border territory.

Letton seems to have been passed by inheritance and marriage at an early date from the Pychards, the Herefordshire family commemorated by the place name Ocle Pychard, and then to the Baskervilles of Eardisley, en route for the Delaberes and Smallmans of Kinnersley. Then on, by way of John Booths, a cavalry officer of Charles I, to John Dutton Colt, Bart, MP for Leominster in 1678. In 1757 the estate was sold to John Freeman of Bristol whose grand-daughter married Joseph Blisset, another Bristolian. He was the father of the Revd Henry Blisset, of whom more will be heard later.

The 17th century Herefordshire antiquary Silas Taylor wrote that:

> Letton is much noted for those excellent grounds....upon the banks of the Wye; the fertility of which are comparable with the Nile, being extraordinary *fatting* grounds.

Letton is still susceptible to flooding, hence the roadside markers for show-ing the depth of the rising waters, but its extent in earlier times is reflected in the area to north of the A438 being known as Letton Lake.

One comes upon Letton parish church as something of a surprise. There is a road-side sign inviting you to turn aside from the A436, go over a small bridge and there, nestling amongst trees, farm buildings, and the squire's Victorian mansion, is the parish church of St John the Baptist. Letton is one of the 500 ancient English dedications to St John the Baptist whose feast on 25th June displaced pagan celebration of the summer solstice. The present chunky building is of stone, under a roof of stone slates. This effect is the result of the chancel being almost as long as the nave, though not so wide, and by there being a south transept, balanced by a north tower. We enter by

119

the Victorian south porch, which protects a Norman doorway, though this belongs to a later church than that used by our Domesday priest. On our visit the door in fact was chained and padlocked, and ironically a smart notice on the nearby notice board prayed:

May God bless you as you visit this church.

Closer observation showed a little yellowing notice on the same board saying the keys may be obtained, amongst other places, at Letton Court Farm Office, but there were no directions as to how to find Letton Court Farm Office. So on this occasion we left, alas, without God's blessing.

The doorway is decorated with zigzag carving up the jambs, and its red sandstone lintel is decorated by a carving of a large central rosette, with several smaller ones on either side. The semi-circular tympanum above the lintel is bare, as if money and inspiration ran out. The door itself is seen as an outstanding example of 12th century craftsmanship, the pattern of its great hinges particularly inspiring the admiration of the *cognoscenti*. There is a smaller door nearby to the south transept. The west door is also Norman with an undecorated tympanum, but the herringbone work on the north wall is a survivor from an earlier church, and may have been familiar to the Domesday priest.

The present chancel was built c.1300, and Pevsner pointed out that the shape of its windows is characteristic of that favoured by the Herefordshire masons of the period. There is an early 14th century south transept and three recesses in the walls for the tombs of local medieval worthies.

But it is the post Reformation furnishings of the church which are its great glory. The Prayer Book laid great emphasis on the importance of the sermon and sound learning, and the Canons of 1602 stated that none should preach unless they were a Bachelor of Divinity, or at least a Master of Arts. Thus for so solemn a responsibility as preaching the pulpit had to reflect the purpose for which it was made whilst fulfilling the practical needs of audibility. The early 18th century Letton pulpit fulfils both requirements, and the tradition that it came originally from a Bristol church is not that unlikely in the light of the fact that both John Freeman and Joseph Blisset had connections with that city.

The pulpit is octagonal and constructed of wood set upon a stone base, which is probably not part of the original structure. It more likely that in its original setting it was set upon an elaborate wooden pedestal and that access to the pulpit was by an elegant curved staircase. All this would have enhanced the sense of occasion and drama associated with the sermon. The tester or sounding board above the pulpit also added to its dignity whilst also helping to project the preacher's voice. The whole structure is decorated with carved festoons of foliage, fruit, and flowers, and a star decorates the underside of the sounding board. There is a reading desk to match.

But despite this emphasis upon the pulpit and the sermon, their importance was not paramount. The pulpit is set to the side of the chancel arch and not at the centre: the focus is on the altar or holy table at the east end of the chancel and the Anglican emphasis is on both word *and* sacrament. At the Reformation stone altars of sacrifice were replaced by wooden tables of communion, of which the Letton table is a good example. Like the pulpit it is enriched with carvings and mouldings and belongs to the late 16th or 17th century. Its ornament, however, was for the glory of God rather than for the sight of man, and the early 17th century canons of the Church of England legislated that the Holy Table should be covered with 'a carpet of silk or other stuff.'

The benches, now in the chancel, belong to the same period as the altar, though their domestic style stands in complete contrast. Their original purpose was for the use of parishioners and they would have stood, with others, in the nave. On the south wall of the chancel a brass memorial commemorates Joane [Parker] who was successively wife of Thomas Dowsing and Edward Chamberlain, rector of Letton, and died in 1697. A second memorial remembers Edward Chamberlain, MA, rector, 1672-1712.

The design and appearance of the church tower at Letton is characteristic of the Marches, though its position at the chancel end of the north side of the nave is less characteristic, despite being repeated, as it is, at Bredwardine. Its stone lower stages, strong and unbuttressed, belong to the mid 14th century, whilst the timber framed top stage, surmounted with its pyramid cap, may be 17th century. Its belfry houses three bells. The treble is early 15th century by R Hendy of Gloucester. It is inscribed *Sancta Madalena* and one wonders whether it originally came from Eardisley parish church, dedicated as it is to St Mary Magadalene, patron of Eardisley. The third bell, late 14th or early 15th century, comes from a Worcester foundry and is inscribed with the Angel's salutation to the Blessed Virgin Mary at the Annunciation: *Maria Gratia plena Dominus tecum,* 'Hail Mary, full of grace, the Lord is with you'. The bells were regularly rung for both religious and secular occasions. In 1866 three new bell ropes from *Simister's Hereford Ropery* in the city's Commercial Street, cost £1 3s 6d.

The maintenance of such churches as this has been dependant over the years on the loyalty and devotion of a succession of churchwardens, of whom little is known, apart from their names. Two wardens were chosen each year at the Easter Vestry, they were not paid for their services, though they could claim for 'their time and trouble'. In 1814 when the roof of Letton church was repaired, Joseph Baker, the churchwarden did much of the work himself, charging the parishioners, through the church rates, £3 7s 0d for his services. This was mainly for hauling timber from Hay on Wye, including the turnpike tolls. Baker charged 2s 0d for picking six bags of moss and 8s 4d, including tolls, for bringing it from Kingswood, on the outskirts of Kington. The roof was being re-tiled and the moss was used for filling the chinks between the tiles. Nails for the job cost £1 14 0d and 2,000 stone tiles were used. It seems that at the same time the interior of the church was painted and limewashed. Seventy bushels of lime were brought from the limekilns at Old Radnor for £2 6s 8d and 'hauling, Turnpikes, and Expence to Limemen' was £1 19 6d. The church was restored in 1883 and it was perhaps then that the plaster was unfortunately removed from the walls, thereby making the building much darker.

Churchwardens also had civil responsibilities, which they shared with the Overseers of the Poor, also elected annually. In December 1744 their Llyswen counterparts in Breconshire complained to the magistrates that a certain Phillip Jones, 'being a poor and impotent person' had sought relief from them. Inquiry revealed, however, that Jones came from Letton and the magistrates decided his relief was a matter for the Letton churchwardens and overseers. They therefore authorized the Llyswen officials to return the unfortunate Jones to Letton at Letton's expense.

Another official of the parish was the Parish Clerk, who was responsible for leading the responses in the services, for keeping the registers, and for putting up official notices. His annual salary in 1865 was £3 12s 9d.

In the 19th century Letton was ruled over by a squarson in the person of the Revd Henry Blisset, MA of Letton Court. Educated at Balliol College, Oxford, he was ordained in 1835 and two years later became rector of the family living of Letton. This meant that Letton now enjoyed a resident incumbent, a privilege it had been denied for some years. In 1833 the Revd Samuel Powell, MA, was licensed as curate of Letton, with a stipend of £63 per annum, together with his surplice fees, and an additional £13 a year from a charity endowed by the wife of a previous patron of the living. He was to live in the rectory and enjoy the use of its garden and offices. He was already a local incumbent and the bishop gave him permission to practice pluralism. The bishop concerned, Dr Edward Grey, bishop of Hereford, 1832-37, was himself an experienced pluralist, besides being the brother of the Prime

Minister, Earl Grey, of tea fame. Sadly the bishop, thrice married, was cut off in his prime at the age of 55, and left behind him a family of 14 children, the youngest of whom was only 18 months old.

When his father died in 1838, Henry Blisset became Lord of the Manor and patron of the adjacent livings of Winforton and Willersley as well as Letton. Of strong Tory sympathies and a member of the Carlton Club, he did not hesitate to try and influence the political sympathies of those amongst his parishioners who had the vote. In July 1852 voting was public and extended over several days and George Cornewall Lewis of Harpton Court, was defending his seat as a Liberal. He lost it in what was an ugly campaign, and James Davies of Moor Court, near Pembridge, a much-respected Kington lawyer and banker, as well as Clerk of the Peace for Radnorshire, sent him a letter of commiseration:

> I rejoice however to hear that you have borne the Disappointment manfully and it is no small Consolation to feel that you have got thro' the Struggle with a very high Degree of Credit in every respect. I must own I should have cared less than I do if we had been beaten by fair means, but the Threats, Bullying, Intimidation, Promises and perhaps a little Bribery have unquestionably stolen from us a large number of votes. I have seen many Contests and never witnessed such Coercion, Force, and Obstruction as did at the Kington Poll and that by persons called Gentleman and Clergyman, whose conduct most certainly was the Cause of what little Disturbance occurred there.

> Parson Blissett was most prominent. On the 1st morning I saw him continually attacking every one of our Color, who was being quickly conducted to the Booth & struggling to get him out of our hands by main force, so that I felt under the disagreeable necessity of telling him pretty freely my opinion and in plain words, publicly, that he was a disgrace to the Church & the Magistracy.

> I was never inclined for the [secret] Ballot until now, and I am now convinced that it is necessary to obtain that or some other improved mode of managing Elections.

In 1863 Blisset rebuilt Letton Court on a new site, nearer the church, the result being what was then thought to be 'a handsome red brick mansion in the medieval style'. For this he engaged the services of the architect Samuel Sanders Teulon, 1812-1873. He favoured what has been described as a 'vigorous and idiosyncratic neo-Gothic style'. This was popular with the landed and wealthy, and Teulon was sought after for the country houses he designed. He was respected not only for his stylistic vigour and inventiveness, but also because he was seen to be a reliable man of business.

At the same time large brick farm buildings were erected nearby the church, and they have a rather more authentic Teulon look than the remodelled Letton Court of the 1920s.

Blisset's widowed mother died in 1867 and Blisset and his family left the rectory for the new big house. However one can never imagine him living in the pretty 16th century black and white house with a gabled two storey porch just west of the churchyard and which was known as *The Old Rectory*. In 1881 he and his wife enjoyed the services of a butler, footman, housekeeper, a lady's maid, housemaid, kitchen maid, under-housemaid, scullery maid, and a coachman who lived over the stables.

The care of souls was now entrusted to new rector for whom in 1870 a large rectory was built in red brick on the Kinnersley road. Blisset also paid for the restoration of Letton church in 1883. Letton Court was destroyed by fire c.1925 and was rebuilt within the Victorian shell and it is uncertain to what degree the present exterior echoes Teulon's original intentions.

Letton in the rain

Walk 7: Kinnersley to Letton and back.

This is a short there-and-back walk taking you to Letton where the church and its unusual setting is well worth a visit. Wellingtons may be more suitable foot wear than walking boots because some of the terrain is rather marshy. Leaving the *Kinnersley Arms*, turn right and walk a short distance down the road until you arrive at a lane on the right-hand side, leading to the hamlet of Ailey. Pass *The Elms* on your right, and the *Masons' Arms* on your left, now a private house, it once served as a post office as well as a public house. Its pedigree probably goes back to the late 16th century.

Pass a farm on the right and the entrance to what looks like a private house on the left. *Old Castle* is on the right. The name suggests that here is the site of the predecessor to Kinnersley Castle, but there is no archaeological evidence to support this. It now looks as if it has been developed as holiday accommodation, showing how the role of an old building can evolve over the centuries.

A finger post on your left-hand side announces that there is now a public footpath on the other side of the rather elaborate wooden fence. There is no stile but the fence is designed to be climbed over. The road itself peters out and carries a *No Exit* sign.

Cross the field to the gate on the other side. Bredwardine Hill lies beyond in the distance. Go through the gate and carry on across the next field. The map will show you that you soon cross another footpath. Two trees stand in the middle of this field, pass between them, and make for the hedge beyond. You come to some steps and a drainage ditch and some more steps give access to a stile beyond it. An arrow on the stile directs you diagonally to your right across the field. A notice asks you to keep to the public right of way.

Arriving at the other side of the field, leave by a double stile on either side of the hedge. An arrow tells you to bear right and go past a little farm house ahead of you, *Lower Kinley*, to which a track gives access, on the right hand side. There is a *Lower* and an *Upper Kinley*. The *–ley* element is locally prevalent in place names, and it has already been remarked how it commemorates a clearing in the woodland, but here at *Kinley* we have a clue as to in *whose*

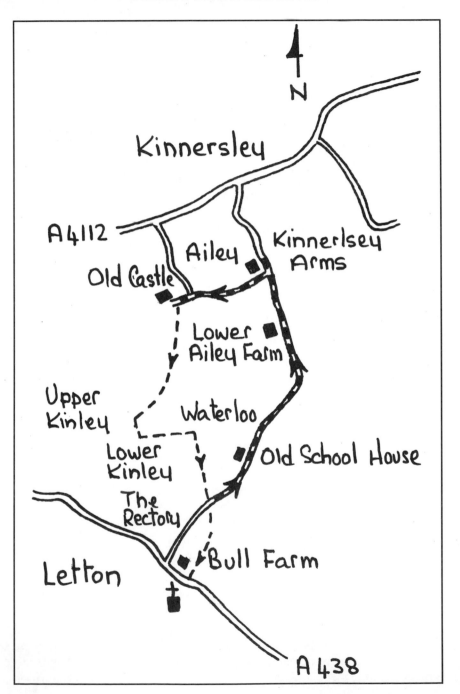

wood the clearing was made. It could be the King's wood, the king being Harold, c.1020-1066, who is also thought to be commemorated in *Kingswood* and *Kington*.

After passing round the back of *Lower Kinley*, continue to bear diagonally left, making for some iron gates in the hedge ahead. Bear left once through the gates, following the hedge until you come to a stile on your left in the corner of the field. Cross this stile, and almost immediately you will see another stile to your right. Cross this stile and the bridge over a drainage ditch. The terrain is now rather marshy, but make for the gap ahead in the hedge in front of you. Pass through the gap which takes you by a bridge over another drainage ditch, and one can see why this area is known as Letton Lake. Make for the pair of oak trees which are slightly to your left and ignore the stile directing you to the left. Instead, turn to your right, and cross the field, heading to the right of the fencing ahead of you. The bogginess of the going is part of its appeal, especially for botanists. Having passed the end of the wire fence, enter the thicket ahead of you. The path is quite well defined and there is a drainage ditch on the other side of the hedge to your right. You will soon see on the right-hand side a bridge with reassuring arrows pointing the way. Cross it and continue on over the field, walking slightly diagonally to your left, making for a large oak tree.

Arriving at the stile, which gives access to the road from Kinnersley to Letton, cross over and then cross the stile facing you by the oak. Bare diagonally right to the hedge and cross another stile and continue across the field. You will see the back of the large Victorian redbrick rectory. The rectory's first occupant was the Revd Thomas Whitley, MA who came from Newton le Willows in 1871. After Liverpool, where he was born, and Newton le Willows, where he worked as a clergyman, with their docks, cotton mills, and collieries, and dense population, he must have found the deeply rural environment of Letton an almost traumatic change. He probably had means, for with the modest stipend of £264 a year, he and his family enjoyed the services of a resident cook, who seems to have come with them from Newton le Willows, and a housemaid. The house is now a private residence, having ceased to be a rectory long ago.

Just where you join the A438 there is a modern farm house to your left, *Bull Farm*. When we did this particular walk in December 2001, Foot and Mouth restrictions still applied to *Bull Farm*. So instead of using the foot path from the ancient oak tree, we remained on the road, and then turned left at the junction with the A438. From here, we walked, quite safely, on the wide grass verge until we arrived opposite the entrance to the drive leading, over a small stone bridge, to Letton Church, which has already been described.

Returning to Kinnersley, retrace your steps to the ancient oak, with the two stiles on opposite sides of the road. But now continue along the road instead of branching off to the left over the stile. This will give you an opportunity to visit the Waterloo nature reserve of the Herefordshire Wild Life Trust. It is part of the *Sturts* SSSI and, although only 3 acres, is rich with wild flowers like the *Great Burnet* which likes a marshy habitat provided by unimproved grassland. In late summer, it produces tiny flowers in compact, slightly arching spikes, which some think resemble bottle-brushes, giving rise to it sometimes being known as the Bottle-Brush Flower.

The Wildlife and Countryside Act of 1981 attempted to address the problem of species protection and habitat loss by, amongst other things, designating Scientific Sites of Special Interest [SSSIs] under the protection of the Nature Conservancy Council. As a result of a legacy the Herefordshire Nature Trust was able to extend its Waterloo Nature Reserve. It remembers the names of those whose generosity made this possible, Geoff and June Smith, by including them in the site's name: The Waterloo Nature Reserve – the Geoff & June Smith Memorial Reserve. The reserves are grazed and visitors should keep to the rights of way.

Continuing along the road to Kinnersley, one passes the old school, now a private house. In its day, 125 years ago, it was presided over by Samuel Norris and his wife Sarah. They both came from Stalybridge in Cheshire, and it was a sign of the times that the education of the children of Letton was in the hands of a 'Certified National School Master' assisted by Sarah who taught the infants. Her mother, a Lancastrian, lived with them and kept house.

On now past *The Valletts* also on the left and the lane giving access to the cluster of cottages called *Waterloo*. The name, of course, commemorates the Duke of Wellington's 1815 victory, and reflects the impact it made even in rural Herefordshire where the French threat was taken as seriously as anywhere. But according to the Royal Commission, there was at least one house here before 1714. In the 19th century agricultural labourers and drainers lived here as well as a master cordwainer, the up-market name for a shoemaker or worker in leather, reflecting once again the self-sufficiency of the rural community which had no catalogues for clothing by mail order.

Then on the left comes *Lower Ailey* farm, now a poultry farm. When Samuel and Sarah Norris were running the school down the road, the farmer at

Lower Ailey supplied him with two daughters and three sons for them to educate. Then there is the turning to Ailey itself with which we began this walk, and lastly the *Kinnersley Arms*, journey's end.

Letton Parish Church

GLOSSARY

Acts of Union: by these acts, passed in 1536 and 1543, the Principality of Wales was annexed to England, and the Marcher Lordships abolished. English law was applied to Wales and five new counties created on the Welsh March. All the Welsh counties were given parliamentary representation.

Advowson: the right, enjoyed by the patron of a living, to appoint the parish priest. Patrons can be individuals, like the lord of the manor, corporate bodies such as Oxbridge colleges, or the Crown.

Alabaster: a fine, white, translucent stone used for sculptured memorials or architectural decoration.

Alb: a white vestment worn by the priest under the chasuble when celebrating mass.

Amice: a square of white linen worn over the shoulders, under the alb, of the priest when celebrating mass.

Apse: the semi-circular end, with an arched roof, sometimes given to church chancels.

Arcadia: a mountainous district in the Peloponnesus, which the ancient world regarded as a setting of ideal rural contentment.

Balusters: a short pear-shaped pillar.

Bargeboard: a board, often carved, fixed beneath of the eaves of a gable and covering the rafters.

Bart: the abbreviation placed after someone's name denoting the person named is a baronet, the lowest hereditary title.

Battered: an architectural term used when the base of a wall deliberately leans inward. It is common in church towers built in a military style avoiding buttresses.

Borough: the settlement which grew up around a castle, and though it paid tolls to the lord of the manor for the right to hold a market, it had a measure of independence. Larger boroughs had the protection of royal charters and were governed by corporations.

Bridle path: a right of way for those travelling on horseback, but not for vehicles, even if horse-drawn.

Burgage plot: the leading townsmen of a borough were called burgesses and their property was called a burgage plot. These plots, because land in the centre of the borough with access to the main street was useful for trade and at a premium, were usually long and narrow.

Canons: the laws of the Church. The canons of the Church of England were ratified by James I in 1603.

Chapel of ease: a chapel built for the convenience of parishioners who live at a distance from the parish church.

Charlemagne: he lived 742-814, and was king of the Franks and Emperor of the Holy Roman Empire. A daughter of Offa, king of Mercia, married one of his sons.

Chasuble: a circular or near circular vestment with a central opening for the head worn by the priest over the alb at mass. The colour of the material varies with the season of the Church's year.

Cruck construction: a style of building in use from the 13th to the 17th centuries, in which pairs of curved timbers were linked together at the top by a ridge pole to form the frame of a building. The method was popular in Wales and the Marches for cottages, farmhouses, and barns.

Cut-waters: the wedge-shaped projections of the piers of a bridge. They divide the current, break up ice floes, and help to prevent debris from blocking the flow of water through the arches of the bridge.

Decorated period: the style of architecture prevailing in the late 13th and 14th centuries. It was characterised by elaborate window tracery and was often imitated by Victorian church architects. It was preceded by the Early English style and followed by the Perpendicular period.

East end/West end: churches where possible, are built along an east-west axis. The east end houses the altar, and the priest when celebrating mass facing the altar, also faces the rising sun, its light shining through the east windows of the chance, symbolizes the resurrection.

Encaustic tiles: these tiles are decorated by inlaying them with patterns formed with different coloured clays before firing them. See also *Godwin tiles*.

Englishry: see *Welshry*.

Equinoctial gales: these occur at the time of the autumn equinox, when day and night are of equal length.

Established Church: the Church of England was established by law as the national church in the 16th century. Its bishops are represented in the House of Lords and it has pastoral responsibilities to the whole population. The Church of England in Wales was disestablished in 1920, and independent of the Crown, it is now known as the Church in Wales.

Godwin tiles: for half a century William and Henry Godwin of Lugwardine, near Hereford, were successful floor tile makers, copying medieval patterns. Examples of their work can be seen in many churches in Herefordshire and Radnorshire. The firm was sold up in 1906.

Jambs: the side posts of doorways and windows.

Jugged hare: a method of cooking a hare, whereby, cut into little pieces, it was put into an earthenware jug and cooked in boiling water.

Lozenge: the diamond shaped shield upon which the arms of a spinster or widow are emblazoned.

Lunette: an architectural term to describe a half-moon shaped window, the base being straight.

Lych-gate: the ceremonial roofed gateway to a churchyard where the introductory part of the funeral service took place. The Old English word *lich* means a corpse.

Meeting House style: early nonconformist chapels were built in a domestic style, deliberately avoiding the ecclesiastical appearance given by the pointed windows and doorways of the gothic style of architecture used in parish churches.

Missal: the altar book containing the text of the mass.

Motte and bailey: a motte was an artificial mound of stone and earth upon which a fort was built, first of wood and then of stone. The bailey was the external defensive wall, again originally of wood, which surrounded the courtyard and motte. This design of castle was introduced to England and Wales by the Normans.

Mullion: the upright separating the lights, or compartments, of a divided window.

National Schools: The National Society for the Education of the Poor in the Principles of the Established Church was founded in 1811 to provide Church schools and to train teachers before the advent of state education. Its nonconformist equivalent was the British and Foreign Schools Society founded in 1807.

Neolithic: the last period of the Stone Age, lasting c. 5000-2400 BC.

OS: the standard abbreviation for the Ordnance Survey. The threat of invasion from France in the late 18th century caused the Board of Ordnance to prepare maps of the south of England on the scale of one inch to the mile. They first map appeared in 1801. Since then high quality maps of the whole country have been produced at various scales and are indispensable for historian and walker alike.

Pall: the ceremonial cloth spread over the coffin at funerals.

Paten: the plate, usually of silver, used with the chalice, or cup, at celebrations of the holy communion.

Pediment: the triangular crown, resembling a low gable, for the front of a building in the classical style.

Peritonitis: inflammation of the membrane lining the abdomen, often fatal before the advent of modern medicine and surgery.

Pilaster: a rectangular pillar, usually actually set in the wall of a building, rather than standing separate as would a column.

Pleached: the custom of pruning and interlacing the branches of a hedge to form a stock proof barrier, offering animals protection from the weather.

RCHM: The Royal Commission on Historical Monuments for over a century has surveyed and recorded English historic buildings and archaeological sites. The National Heritage Act of 1983 set up the Historic Buildings and Monuments Commission for England and the two bodies later merged to become English Heritage, and is entrusted with conserving and making the nation's built heritage more accessible to the public.

Rector: historically the title given to a parson or incumbent of a parish who received all his tithes and none of them were appropriated to other recipients. Though nowadays there is no practical distinction between a rector and a vicar, recently the title has also been applied to the leader of a team ministry. See also *Vicar* and *tithes*.

Reredos: the screen, often sculptured, covering the wall above the back of the altar.

Sheriff: the sheriff was the chief official of a county in Norman times, but his duties were gradually taken over by the Justices of the Peace and the Lord Lieutenant. Vestiges of the office survive in that of the High Sheriff, appointed for each county annually.

Simony: the illegal practice of buying ecclesiastical appointments.

Stucco: the name given to the special plaster used for facing external walls.

Squarson: a title formed from combination of *squire* and *parson*, used for a clergyman who is also the squire of his parish.

Surplice: the white and very full vestment worn by clergymen and choristers during church services.

Surplice fees: for wedding and funeral services the clergyman wears a surplice, and because he was entitled to a fee for performing such services, these were known as *surplice fees.*

Tithes: the Church took over the Biblical injunction that one-tenth of the produce of the land should be set aside for the work of God. From the eighth century the tithes of the parishioners went to support the rector of the parish who in return was responsible for maintaining the chancel of the parish church and for providing their spiritual care. Though originally paid in kind, tithes were later received as a money payment. A great cause of dissension and resentment, they did not finally disappear until 1996.

Tractarian: the title given to a clergyman agreeing with the religious principles first laid down in a series of 90 pamphlets called *Tracts for the Times,* published 1833-41. These tracts emphasized the historical continuity of the Church of England with the early Church and advocated the greater use of ceremonial in the Prayer Book services.

Transhumance: the ancient practice whereby livestock which had wintered in the sheltered lowlands were taken to upland pastures for the summer, their shepherds and herdsmen living with them. The custom is commemorated in Welsh place names by *Hendre,* the old or winter dwelling, and *Hafod,* the summer dwelling.

Transom: the lintel or cross beam in a mullioned window.

Tympanum: the name given to the panel above a door and beneath the arch above it. It was often decorated with sculpture or carving in medieval churches.

Vicar: the vicar was a clergyman, usually appointed by an absentee rector to look after the spiritual life of a parish. Nowadays there is no practical difference between a vicar or rector of a parish, and which title he has is a matter of the parish's past history. See *Rector*.

Welshry: The part of the land, inhabited by both the English and the Welsh, to which the native Welsh were confined. The part inhabited by the English was the Englishry.

Windlass: a machine used for hauling barges by winding chains or ropes attached to them around a drum.

Window tax: a tax introduced in 1697 and abolished in 1851 whereby the occupier of a house was taxed according to the number of windows in their house.

BIBLIOGRAPHY

Anon. *The Trial, Conviction, and Condemnation of Andrew Brommich and William Atkins for being Romish Priests*, London, 1679.

Steven Bassett, ed., *The Origins of Anglo-Saxon Kingdoms*, Leicester, 1989.

Kenneth Cameron, *English Place-names*, 3rd edition, London, 1977.

KR Clew, *Kilvert's Bredwardine*, Bredwardine, 1980

KR Clew, *Bredwardine, Hereford. A brief guide,* Bredwardine. 1981.

KR Clew, *Kinnersley, Herefordshire*, Kinnersley, 1998.

FL Cross, ed, *The Oxford Dictionary of the Christian Church*, Oxford, 1958.

Eilert Ekwall, *The Concise Oxford Dictionary of English Place-names*, 4th edition, Oxford, 1960.

HPR Finberg, *The Early Charters of the West Midlands*, Leicester, 1961.

HPR Finberg, *Lucerna*, London, 1964.

Foster, *Alumni Oxoniensis,*

Margaret Gelling, *The West Midlands in the Early Middle Ages*, Leicester, 1992.

David Gorvett, *The Parish Church of St Mary Magdalene, Eardisley*, Eardisley, 1993.

David Gorvett, 'Church Restoration -Then and Now', *Kington History Society Papers, 1996-97.*

David Hey, ed, *The Oxford Companion to Local and Family History*, Oxford 1998.

Robert Jenkins, *A Brief History of the Church and Parish of Almeley*, Kington, 1991.

Samuel Lewis, *A Topographical Dictionary of England*, four volumes, London, 1831.

J Littelbury, *Directory and Gazetteer of Herefordshire*, Worcester, 1876.

L Lumsdon, *Mortimer Trail Walker's Guide*, Worcester, 1997.

RCB Oliver, 'The Shelleys of Radnorshire', *Transactions of the Radnorshire Society*, Vol XLI, 1971.

Richard Pantall, *George Jarvis and his Notorious Charity*, Hereford, 1993.

Richard Parry, *The History of Kington*, Kington, 1845.

N Pevsner, *The Buildings of England: Herefordshire*, Harmondsworth, 1963.

LMR Potter, *The History of the Hamlet of Bollingham in the parish of Eardisley, Herefordshire*, published privately, 1993-6.

Michael Raven, *A Guide to Herefordshire*, published privately, 1996.

Peter Reid, *Burke's & Savills Guide to Country Houses*, Vol II, Herefordshire, Shropshire, Warwickshire, Worcestershire, London , 1980.

CJ Robinson, *A History of the Castles of Herefordshire and their Lords,* London, 1869.

CJ Robinson, *A History of the Mansions and Manors of Herefordshire,* London, 1872.

Royal Commission on Historical Monuments England: An Inventory of the Historical Monuments in Herefordshire, Vol 3, London, 1934.

Mike Salter, *The Castles of Herefordshire and Worcestershire,* Wolverhampton, 1989.

Mike Salter, *The Old Parish Churches of Herefordshire*, Wolverhampton, 1990.

Michael Sharp, *From Compostela to Kinnersley*, Kinnersley, 1998.

Michael Sharp, *Kinnersley and the Bodley Connection*, Kinnersley, 1999.

Ron Shoesmith, *Castles and Moated Sites of Herefordshire*, Logaston, 1996.

JB Sinclair & RWD Fenn, *The Facility of Locomotion*, Kington, 1991.

JB Sinclair & RWD Fenn, *History and Landscape: Twelve Country walks from Kington*, Kington, 1995.

Joan and Harold Taylor, 'Pre-Norman Churches of the Border', *Celt and Saxon, Studies in the Early British Border,* Cambridge, 1964.

Venn, *Alumni Cantabrigensis*, Cambridge, 1922.

David Verey, *Herefordshire. A Shell Guide*, London, 1955.

E Walford, *The County Families of the United Kingdom*, London, 1873.

WR Williams, *Herefordshire Members 1213-1896,* Brecon, 1896.

Wye Valley Walk, Worcester, 1996.

INDEX

Abel, John, King's Carpenter, 9, 12, 13,
Aberffraw, Anglesey, 38
Acts of Union, 89
Adam, Robert, architect, 90
Agincourt, Battle of, 1415, 91
Agriculture, 46, 47
Agricultural accidents, 61
Ailey, 81, 125
Aldworth, the Revd W St Ledger, of
    Eardisley, 108
Alexander, Mrs, Hymn writer, 83
Almeley, 29
    Almeley House, 37
    Castle, 26, 29, 30, 39, 111
    Castle Frome Farm, 38
    Church, 30, 31, 32, 33, 91
    Church House, 37, 48
    Fish ponds, 30
    Frome stream, 39, 111
    Manor Cottage, 37
    Manor House, 37
    Mill Orchard, 38
    New Inn, 27
    Newport, see Newport Almeley
    Old Castle, see Castle
    Old Vicarage, 27, 33
    Primary School, 48
    Railway station, 36, 40, 45
    Station Farm, 40
    Summer House, 26
    The Bells, 27, 32, 37, 48, 65, 111
    Upcot, 29
    War memorial, 37, 48
Almeley place-name 29
Almeley Wootton, 26
    Quaker Meeting House, 26
Andrews, the Revd Frederick, of
    Kinnersley, 74, 75, 76
Apples, 116
Archenfield, 89
Ariconium, 89
Arrow Masonic Lodge, 17
Arrow river, 7, 21, 118
Arthur's Stone, 102, 103

Badham, William, of Bollingham, 110
Banks family, 8, 13, 19, 22, 23, 80
Baird, Henry, Almeley, 27
Baker, Joseph, Letton churchwarden, 122
Bards, 7
Barnesley family, 50, 51, 52, 54
Barnwell, EL, archaeologist, 102, 103
Baskerville family, 49, 50, 55, 90, 91, 119
Baynham, Richard, of Aston Ingham, 78
Beaven, Naomi, of Eardisley Station, 63
Bevington, organ builder, 73
Black Mountains, 1, 48, 65, 111, 113, 114
Blessed Virgin Mary, dedications to, 30
Blisset family of Letton, 119, 120, 122,
    123, 124
Bodley, Frederick, 1827-1907, architect,
    56, 75, 76
Bollingham, 58
    Cambrian visit, 107, 108
    Castle, 107
    Chapel of ease, 107, 108, 109, 113,
    114
    Dedication to St Silas, 107
    Domesday entry, 107
    Place-name entry, 107
Bollingham House, 110
Bosworth, Reuben, Nottingham clock-
    maker, 57
Bradnor Hill, 7
Brecon Beacons, 1, 111, 113
Breconshire Coal and Lime Company, 81
Bredwardine, 26, 85
    Bridge, 88, 95
    Castle, 90
    Church, 90, 91, 92, 93
    Churchyard, 105
    Cockfighting, 99
    Crafta Webb, 93, 101, 102
    Dedication to St Andrew, 90
    Domesday entry 89
    Fishponds, 90
    Floods, 95, 96
    Light railway proposals, 97
    Occupations, 97